Business Management IN THE Local Church

Business Management

IN THE

Local Church

David R. Pollack

MOODY PRESS

CHICAGO

Contents

Foreword   7

Introduction   9

1. Sharpening the Vision of the Local Church   11

2. Church and Law   15

3. Introduction to Church Finances   41

4. Fundamentals of Budgeting   69

5. Budgeting and Forecasting—Beyond the Basics   87

6. How to Turn Around a Financially Troubled Church   111

7. Workers Worthy of Hire   121

8. Facilities Management   139

9. Managing the Risks   147

10. Is the Way We Give Hurting Our Church?   153

11. Hey, Brother, Can You Spare a Dime?   157

12. Worthy Is the Pastor   161

Foreword

For many years I have been dismayed by the lack of good, biblical information on church financial administration. With his expanded *Business Management in the Local Church*, Dave Pollock has stepped in and "filled the gap." This manual is packed with practical —and profoundly useful—guidelines for the management of church finances.

Whenever Dave has appeared on our radio program *Money Matters*, I've been amazed at the wisdom he has been able to apply in the often volatile arena of the stewardship of church funds. I can heartily recommend this book to pastors, administrators, and laymen alike, and I am pleased that the tremendous needs our churches face with regard to church financial administration have at last been expertly addressed.

LARRY BURKETT
CHRISTIAN FINANCIAL CONCEPTS

Introduction

The management of resources within the local church is rapidly becoming one of the more significant challenges facing church leaders today. Operating churches in an organized, efficient, and effective manner isn't nearly as simple as it once was. That is because of growing public awareness, increased governmental scrutiny, and the recognition on the part of church leaders in general that improvements in managing church finances must be made.

The basic mission of the church today has not changed from that of the first-century body of believers—it is to evangelize, equip, and care for the flock. A major difference, however, is the type—and use—of the physical resources placed at our disposal to accomplish that task.

The operation of a church is, in many respects, quite similar to that of a business. Even though the local church is not in business to make a profit, it is still a business—the Lord's business. Therefore, to have the respect of the community in which it serves, and thus an effective testimony, it is essential that churches use good business methods. The apostle Paul's statement in 1 Corinthians 14:40, "Let all things be done decently and in order," certainly applies to the temporal aspects of a church as well as to its worship procedures.

Sharpening the Vision of the Local Church

Y ou're trying to run the church like a corporation" was heard when it was suggested that the church form a Long-Range Planning Committee. In the past, concerns were often voiced about the loss of flexibility or spontaneity when formal goal-setting procedures were proposed. But whereas the concept of strategic planning may have been considered a luxury that only large ministries could afford to be involved in, today it is a necessity for all churches—large or small.

A recent survey[1] showed that in the area of short-range planning 92 percent of large churches (five hundred or more members) had one-year plans, whereas 77 percent of the smaller churches polled had a formal, written, twelve-month strategy. However, when the question of long-range (three to five year) planning was asked, the figures plunged to 42 percent for the large and 14 percent for the small churches.

Two primary arguments are often raised against strategic planning and budgeting: unforeseen changes in the economy, and overcontrol.

Objections to Long-Range Planning

Changing Economic Conditions

Changes in the economy in the form of recessions, inflation, and rising interest rates, all can affect the church collection plate. The impact is especially felt when economic conditions cause a decrease in giving. For instance, a church located in a suburban community could experience a drop in contributions if home mortgage interest rates were to increase. Those families on variable mortgage rates would have less spendable income.

1. R. Henry Migloire, Oral Roberts University, Tulsa, Oklahoma (1986).

The issue here isn't whether it is right or wrong for people to cut back on their giving. The point is that there could be less money available to carry out some of the church's plans. It is important, therefore, to develop within the budgeting process both positive and negative scenarios. With the introduction of computerized, electronic spreadsheets, the "what ifs" of budgeting can be reduced to hard-copy black-and-white.

Therefore, a 10 percent increase in giving or a 7 percent reduction, for instance, can be calculated selectively or across the board to all budgeted departments. The effects of increased or decreased giving could be applied to any or all ministries of the church, from one month to one decade.

A changing economy doesn't mean that planning can't go forward and be effective.

Overcontrol

The second objection to long-range planning is that it could place a choke-hold on creativity or flexibility. This argument can be valid in many cases—not right, but valid. Often the budget becomes chiseled in stone and new opportunities get shot down because "they're not in the budget."

I'm not advocating throwing financial projections out the window or "busting" the budget with overspending. However, there is no reason line-items can't be moved around or projects with a lesser priority set aside in the interest of a new opportunity. Flexibility is the key to overcoming this drawback to strategic planning.

Long-range planning is the blueprint of the church's future, showing where the church expects to be after a given period of time. This blueprint is usually in the form of a game plan, complete with projections of income, personnel, space, facility requirements, and other significant factors that affect church growth. These long-range projections are based on past performance and assumptions about the future and are normally projected three to five years into the future.

It should be understood that budgeting is a result of long-range planning and should fall in behind the strategic plan—not come before it. First comes the plan, then comes the identification of needed resources.

Five Characteristics of Long-Range Plans

1. *Identification*—Long-term goals are identified by asking, "Where does the church want to go?"
2. *Potential*—Church leadership is alerted to the potential opportunities and risks before they occur, thus allowing the church to take advantage of the opportunities and avoid the risks.

3. *Projections*—After goals are identified, the long-range plan projects future financial requirements, people needs, and other resource necessities.

4. *Alternatives*—Alternative courses of action can be formulated to reach the goals. Each course of action should be evaluated. This begins the process of selecting those alternatives that are most feasible in light of the church's resources.

5. *Review*—Long-range planning provides a framework for periodic review so that a church can measure its progress and, when necessary, make modifications.

"It is important to remember that long-range planning is, to a large extent, based on short-term planning. Any long-range planning not based on the church's current functional plan is an exercise in futility. Conversely, to maximize results and prevent leaders and staff from going in all directions, functional plans must be integrated into one, unified, long-range plan."[2]

Since planning deals with the unknown, once again it should be reemphasized that a strategic plan needs to be *flexible*. And while a long-range plan cannot guarantee success, it can certainly help a church bring current problems under control, overcome future obstacles, and maximize its potential for effectiveness.

2. *Strategic Planning* (Monterey, Calif.: Business Research & Communications, 1986), p. 8.

Section 2

Church and Law

Christ established it, He died for it, and He promised us that the very gates of hell could not conquer it. For the believer, that is a well-known, comforting, and unmistakable fact.

Secular society, on the other hand, has different ideas about the church. Without question, throughout history the true biblical church has often been the subject of scorn and persecution, and sometimes it has simply been ignored.

So far the North American church has not had to endure many of the hardships experienced by others throughout history. Perhaps our day is coming. In fact, there *are* signs that our secular society is losing its tolerance for the church. Federal, state, and local laws are being passed that continue to restrict and, in some instances, inhibit the activities of local churches.

Church leaders need to be aware of how they are viewed in the eyes of the law in order to avoid problems and complications with the "system." The days of cloaking church activities under the protective mantle of the First Amendment or other constitutional interpretations of freedom of religion are disappearing. Therefore, within the context of society's changing perceptions, how should the church position itself in today's legal and legislative environment?

Generally speaking—and for our purposes—a church by definition has two meanings. First, there is the physical description: "a building set apart or consecrated for public worship." Then there is the people-oriented designation: "a group of worshipers: a congregation."[3]

A legal definition could also encompass both of these definitions. When a group of worshipers who call themselves a church wish to officially establish themselves as a "church," there are two choices facing them right away. Should a church be a nonprofit corporation or an unincorporated association? Legally, a church is not required

3. *Webster's New World Dictionary*, 2d ed. (New York: Simon & Schuster, 1980).

to become incorporated. However, there are certain advantages available to the members if they do choose to incorporate.

Incorporation

The main advantages of incorporation are liability protection and tax exemption. A church that chooses to do business as a corporation has protection from liability. Members are exempt from liability if the leaders or other members engage in any wrongful activity. In the event of a legal judgment against the church, claims would be paid out of an insurance policy or from the assets of the church—but not from assets of the members. If an individual officer or person is guilty of wrongdoing, a lawsuit could be brought against that individual, but the remaining members would be free from liability.

The disadvantages of not incorporating are significant. Although some churches refuse to become "entangled" in governmental regulations on philosophical grounds, perhaps they should reconsider their decision.

On a practical level, it is difficult to do business without incorporating. Banks are reluctant to open accounts without someone's taking ultimate responsibility, which usually means the senior pastor. A church functioning as an unincorporated association normally places the pastor or one or more trustees at risk for all debts, contracts, and legal matters. Furthermore, while an unincorporated church cannot sue or be sued, in most states legal action can be brought against the church members.

Governmental Benefits of Incorporating

When a church incorporates, it normally secures a nonprofit status. The benefits of a nonprofit distinction are many. Federal statutes provide certain direct benefits to nonprofit corporations.

- A nonprofit may apply and receive exemption from federal income taxes.
- In some instances, a nonprofit may receive a reduced postal rate.

On a state level, nonprofits enjoy certain other benefits:

- Exemption from state income taxes
- Release from paying franchise taxes
- Exemption from property taxes

When applying for nonprofit, tax-exempt status under federal law, churches usually must receive a nonprofit status from their state government. Once this is accomplished, a church would apply for the status of a public charity and the designation as a "501 (c)(3)" organization. This 501 (c)(3) classification affects both the activities that the organization may engage in and the manner in which contributions will be treated.

The Internal Revenue Code defines and sets forth guidelines and qualifications for a nonprofit corporation. These include the drafting of Articles of Incorporation and By-laws. These documents lay out the legal structure of the church government along with certain limitations on activities. It is advisable either to secure the services of an attorney when preparing these documents or to thoroughly research the preparation of the text at a local library. Generally speaking, to secure the 501 (c)(3) status from the federal government, your Articles of Incorporation must include the following:

1. A "Religious Purpose" clause
2. A clause that states that there will be no "Propaganda or Political Activity"
3. A method for disbanding the corporation or a "Provision for Dissolution Clause"

Once the church has satisfactorily met all the government's requirements, a letter of determination will be issued from the IRS confirming the 501 (c)(3) status.

It is interesting to note that a church is not required to incorporate in order to gain tax-exempt status from the federal government. However, the issues of protection from liability and other corporate benefits should be considered. There are churches that have chosen not to file for 501 (c)(3) status on theological grounds. The primary disadvantage of not being considered a 501 (c)(3) exempt organization is that if a contributor should be audited by the IRS in connection with his or her charitable donations, the church might, on behalf of the donor, be required to prove it substantially meets the IRS criteria. Once a church goes through this process a few times, it might wish to reconsider its objection to federal recognition.

Governmental Requirements

Reporting

Though some of the reporting requirements will be touched on briefly in this section, each church should use a competent CPA who is well acquainted with tax laws as they relate specifically to churches. This cannot be stressed strongly enough.

County

It may be necessary to comply with county or local property tax laws if you have been exempted from property tax. This is normally done on an annual basis.

State

Many states require churches to file a form on an annual basis informing them of the names of the church's officers as well as the individual to contact for legal purposes. This is often done through the State Corporation Commission or Secretary of State.

There are other requirements for churches that could involve Workman's Compensation Insurance. However, in most states the church is exempt from paying unemployment taxes. Moreover, state disability taxes vary in different states.

There may be additional forms to file if your employees are subject to state (also city and county) income taxes.

Federal

If the church is an employer, it is subject to state and federal labor, withholding, and other tax laws. Compliance is required—not an option—and protection as a "church" is not assured. There are several forms that relate to the area of taxation that church financial leaders need to be familiar with.

IRS Form 8274	Deals with Social Security tax for church employers. (See Exhibit 2-1.)
IRS Form 4361	Relates to Social Security and ministers. (See Exhibit 2-2.)
IRS Form 941 or 941E	These forms are for the reporting of city, state, or federal tax withholding. If the church is exempt from Social Security, 941E is to be submitted. (See Exhibits 2-3, 2-4.)
IRS Form W-4	Pertains to all employees and some minister employees. (See Exhibit 2-5.)
IRS Form W-2	This form is a statement of earnings. (See Exhibit 2-6.)
IRS Form W-3	Sent to the Social Security Administration and, in some instances, to the state. (See Exhibit 2-7.)
IRS Form 1099 MISC.	Issued to self-employed individuals. (See Exhibit 2-8.)
IRS Form 1099 INT.	Issued to anyone to whom the church paid interest of more than $10 in a calendar year. (See Exhibit 2-9.)

IRS Form 1096	This is a transmittal form for all 1099 forms. The church should determine state requirements. (See Exhibit 2-10.)
IRS Form 5578	Every 501 (c)(3) organization operating a private school must file this form annually. (See Exhibit 2-11.)
IRS Form 8283	This form is submitted to the IRS for donations of noncash items in excess of $500 or less than $5,000. Read it carefully. (See Exhibit 2-12.)
IRS Form 8282	To be completed by the church only if non-cash items are sold. (See Exhibit 2-13.)
IRS Form 8300	If a church (or any other ministry) receives $10,000 or more in cash in any business or trade transaction (e.g., rental of property or a parking lot), it would need to be reported on Form 8300. (See Exhibit 2-14.)
IRS Form W-9	This form needs to be completed by a visiting ministry or other independent contractor in the event a Form 1099 should be required for these people at a later date. (See Exhibit 2-15.)
IRS Form I-9	The Immigration and Naturalization Service requires this to be on file for every employee. (See Exhibit 2-16.)
IRS Form 990	A church is not obligated to fill out and return this form. (See Exhibit 2-17.)
IRS Form 990T	A church that receives $1,000 or more in gross income from an unrelated trade or business must file this form. (See Exhibit 2-18.)
IRS Form 1040ES	This form is to be filled out by a minister on a quarterly basis for their estimated federal income and SECA taxes.[4] (See Exhibit 2-19.)

Churches should seek the advice of a qualified CPA in these matters, since most of these forms require further in-depth understanding. There may also be additional requirements if a church employs a number of people who are engaged in trade or commerce, or are doing business in other states.

4. Don L. Buckel and Barbara E. Buckel, *The Church Administration "How To" Manual* (Lakeside, Calif.), 1990.

Privileges with Accountability

Although it may seem like the government places a lot of burdensome rules and regulations on churches, it should all be kept in perspective. On balance, no other nation in the world provides as many benefits and exemptions for religious organizations as does the United States. Sometimes we forget some of the freedoms granted to our churches.

Christ certainly recognized the distinction between political and spiritual responsibilities when He said, "Give unto Caesar what is Caesar's and to God what is God's" (Matthew 22:21, NIV*). As long as the laws do not inhibit clear and unmistakable biblical teaching regarding the mission and mandate of the local church, churches need to cooperate with the government and obey the rules.

*New International Version.

Form **8274**
(Rev. December 1989)

Department of the Treasury
Internal Revenue Service

Certification by Churches and Qualified Church-Controlled Organizations Electing Exemption From Employer Social Security Taxes

File in Duplicate

Please type or print		
Full name of organization		Employer identification number
Address (number and street)		
City, state, and ZIP code		Date wages first paid
If exemption is based on a group ruling, give full name of central organization		Group exemption number

Purpose of Form.—By filing this form, the organization named above elects exemption from employer social security taxes by certifying that it is a church or church-controlled organization which is opposed for religious reasons to the payment of social security taxes.

Effect of Election.—This election applies to all current and future employees of the electing organization for services performed. However, this election does not apply to ministers of a church, members of a religious order, or to services performed in an unrelated trade or business of the church or church-controlled organization.

The electing organization is required to continue to withhold income tax and to report the tax withheld and wages, tips, and other compensation paid to each employee on **Form W-2,** Wage and Tax Statement, and to file **Form 941E,** Quarterly Return of Withheld Federal Income Tax and Hospital Insurance (Medicare) Tax (or **Form 941,** Employer's Quarterly Federal Tax Return, if the organization has employees whose wages are not exempted by this election, such as those engaged in unrelated business activities, and remain subject to employer taxes). The organization can permanently revoke the election by filing Form 941 and paying social security taxes. This election will be permanently revoked if the organization fails to file Form W-2 for 2 years or more and fails to furnish such information within 60 days after a written request by the IRS.

Employees receiving compensation of $100 or more in a year from the electing organization are subject to self-employment tax on the compensation. They will be considered employees for all other purposes of the Internal Revenue Code including the withholding of income tax.

Who May File.—Churches and qualified church-controlled organizations (defined below) who are opposed for religious reasons to the payment of social security taxes, may elect exemption from the taxes by filing this form.

The term "church" means a church described in section 501(c)(3) and section 170(b)(1)(A)(i) of the Internal Revenue Code. The term "church" includes conventions or associations of churches. It also includes an elementary or secondary school that is controlled, operated, or

principally supported by a church (or conventions or associations of churches).

A qualified church-controlled organization includes any church-controlled tax-exempt organization described in section 501(c)(3) of the Internal Revenue Code except an organization that:

1. Offers goods, services, or facilities for sale, other than on an incidental basis, to the general public, AND

2. Normally receives more than 25% of its support from the sum of governmental sources and receipts from admissions, sales of merchandise, or furnishing of facilities in activities that are related trades or businesses.

Goods, services, or facilities which are sold at a nominal charge substantially less than the cost of providing such goods, services, or facilities are not included in condition 1 above.

An organization which meets both conditions 1 and 2 above will be excluded from the definition of a qualified church-controlled organization and therefore not eligible to file this form. For example a church-controlled hospital will generally meet both conditions and will not qualify to make the election.

However, a seminary, a religious retreat center, or a burial society will generally qualify to make the election regardless of its funding sources because it does not offer goods, services, or facilities for sale to the general public. A church-run orphanage or home for the aged may qualify if not more than 25% of its support is from admissions, sales of merchandise, or furnishing of facilities in other than unrelated trades or businesses plus from governmental sources. Auxiliary organizations of a church such as youth groups, women's auxiliaries, church pension boards, and fund-raising organizations will generally be eligible to make the election.

When To File.—File this form in duplicate after you hire employees but prior to the first date on which a quarterly employment tax return would otherwise be due from the electing organization.

Where To File.—File with the Internal Revenue Service Center for the state in which the church or church-controlled organization is located, as listed.

Florida, Georgia, South Carolina	Atlanta, GA 39901
New Jersey, New York (New York City and counties of Nassau, Rockland, Suffolk, and Westchester)	Holtsville, NY 00501
New York (all other counties), Connecticut, Maine, Massachusetts, New Hampshire, Rhode Island, Vermont	Andover, MA 05501
Illinois, Iowa, Minnesota, Missouri, Wisconsin	Kansas City, MO 64999
Delaware, District of Columbia, Maryland, Pennsylvania, Virginia	Philadelphia, PA 19255
Indiana, Kentucky, Michigan, Ohio, West Virginia	Cincinnati, OH 45999
Kansas, New Mexico, Oklahoma, Texas	Austin, TX 73301
Alaska, Arizona, California (counties of Alpine, Amador, Butte, Calaveras, Colusa, Contra Costa, Del Norte, El Dorado, Glenn, Humboldt, Lake, Lassen, Marin, Mendocino, Modoc, Napa, Nevada, Placer, Plumas, Sacramento, San Joaquin, Shasta, Sierra, Siskiyou, Solano, Sonoma, Sutter, Tehama, Trinity, Yolo, and Yuba), Colorado, Idaho, Montana, Nebraska, Nevada, North Dakota, Oregon, South Dakota, Utah, Washington, Wyoming	Ogden, UT 84201
California (all other counties), Hawaii	Fresno, CA 93888
Alabama, Arkansas, Louisiana, Mississippi, North Carolina, Tennessee	Memphis, TN 37501

Churches or church-controlled organizations in Guam, the Commonwealth of the Northern Mariana Islands, American Samoa, the Virgin Islands, or Puerto Rico should file this form with the U.S. Internal Revenue Service Center, Philadelphia, PA 19255.

If you are a current Form 941 filer, file Form 8274 with the Internal Revenue Service Center where you file Form 941.

Filing Instructions.—Complete this form by providing the information requested. If you do not have an employer identification number, submit a completed **Form SS-4,** Application for Employer Identification Number, with this election. If you have applied for a number but have not yet received it, write "Applied for" and the date you applied in the space provided for the number. An authorized official of the church or the qualified church-controlled organization must sign the form. Send two copies to the appropriate IRS address. Keep a copy for your records.

Sign Here ▶

I certify that the above named organization is a church or qualified church-controlled organization which, as defined in section 3121(w) of the Internal Revenue Code, is opposed for religious reasons to the payment of employer social security taxes, and elects not to be subject to such taxes.

-------------------------------- (Signature of authorized official)   -------------------------------- (Title)   -------------------------------- (Date)

Exhibit 2-1

Form **4361**
(Rev. June 1991)
Department of the Treasury
Internal Revenue Service

Application for Exemption From Self-Employment Tax for Use by Ministers, Members of Religious Orders and Christian Science Practitioners

OMB No. 1545-0168
Expires 6-30-94

File Original and Two Copies

File original and two copies and attach supporting documents. This exemption is granted only if the IRS returns a copy to you marked "approved."

Please type or print

1 Name of taxpayer shown on Form 1040	Social security number
Number and street (including apt. no.)	Telephone number (optional) ( )
City or town, state, and ZIP code	

2 Check ONE box: ☐ Christian Science practitioner ☐ Ordained minister, priest, rabbi
☐ Member of religious order not under a vow of poverty ☐ Commissioned or licensed minister (see line 6)

3 Date ordained, licensed, etc. (Attach supporting document. See instructions.)
/ /

4 Legal name of ordaining, licensing, or commissioning body or religious order

Number, street, and room or suite no.

Employer identification number

City or town, state, and ZIP code

5 Enter the first 2 years, after the date shown on line 3, that you had net self-employment earnings of $400 or more, any of which came from services as a minister, priest, rabbi, etc.; member of a religious order; or Christian Science practitioner ▶   19 _____   19 _____

6 If you apply for the exemption as a licensed or commissioned minister, and your denomination also ordains ministers, please indicate how your ecclesiastical powers differ from those of an ordained minister of your denomination. Attach a copy of your denomination's by-laws relating to the powers of ordained, commissioned, or licensed ministers.

7 I certify that I am conscientiously opposed to, or because of my religious principles I am opposed to, the acceptance (for services I perform as a minister, member of a religious order not under a vow of poverty, or a Christian Science practitioner) of any public insurance that makes payments in the event of death, disability, old age, or retirement; or that makes payments toward the cost of, or provides services for, medical care. (Public insurance includes insurance systems established by the Social Security Act.)

I certify that as a duly ordained, commissioned, or licensed minister of a church or a member of a religious order not under a vow of poverty, I have informed the ordaining, commissioning, or licensing body of my church or order that I am conscientiously opposed to, or because of religious principles, I am opposed to the acceptance (for services I perform as a minister or as a member of a religious order) of any public insurance that makes payments in the event of death, disability, old age, or retirement; or that makes payments toward the cost of, or provides services for, medical care, including the benefits of any insurance system established by the Social Security Act.

I certify that I did not file an effective waiver certificate (Form 2031) electing social security coverage on earnings as a minister, member of a religious order not under a vow of poverty, or a Christian Science practitioner.

I request to be exempted from paying self-employment tax on my earnings from services as a minister, member of a religious order not under a vow of poverty, or a Christian Science practitioner, under section 1402(e) of the Internal Revenue Code. I understand that the exemption, if granted, will apply only to these earnings. Under penalties of perjury, I declare that I have examined this application and to the best of my knowledge and belief, it is true and correct.

Signature ▶   Date ▶

Caution: Form 4361 is **not proof** of the right to an exemption from Federal income tax withholding or social security tax, the right to a parsonage allowance exclusion (section 107), assignment by your religious superiors to a particular job, or the exemption or church status of the ordaining, licensing, commissioning body, or religious order.

For Internal Revenue Service Use

☐ Approved for exemption from self-employment tax on ministerial earnings
☐ Disapproved for exemption from self-employment tax on ministerial earnings

By ....
(Director's signature)   (Date)

General Instructions

(Section references are to the Internal Revenue Code.)

Paperwork Reduction Act Notice.—We ask for the information on this form to carry out the Internal Revenue laws of the United States. You are required to give us the information. We need it to ensure that you are complying with these laws and to allow us to figure and collect the right amount of tax.

The time needed to complete and file this form will vary depending on individual circumstances. The estimated average time is:

Recordkeeping, 7 minutes; **Learning about the law or the form,** 19 minutes; **Preparing the form,** 16 minutes; **Copying, assembling, and sending the form to IRS,** 17 minutes.

If you have comments concerning the accuracy of these time estimates or suggestions for making this form more simple, we would be happy to hear from you. You can write to both the **Internal Revenue Service,** Washington, DC 20224, Attention: IRS Reports Clearance Officer, T:FP; and the **Office of Management and Budget,** Paperwork Reduction Project (1545-0168), Washington, DC 20503. **DO NOT** send the form to either of these offices. Instead, see **Where To File** on page 2.

Purpose of Form.—File Form 4361 to apply for an exemption from self-employment tax if you are:

● An ordained, commissioned, or licensed minister of a church;

● A member of a religious order who has not taken a vow of poverty;

● A Christian Science practitioner; or

● A commissioned or licensed minister of a church or church denomination that ordains ministers, if you have authority to perform substantially all religious duties of your church or denomination.

This application must be based on your religious or conscientious opposition to the acceptance (for services performed as a minister, member of a religious order, or Christian Science practitioner) of any public insurance that makes payments for death, disability, old age, or retirement; or that makes payments for the cost of, or provides services for, medical care, including any insurance benefits established by the Social Security Act.

If you are a duly ordained, commissioned, or licensed minister of a church or a member of a religious order not under a vow of poverty, prior to filing this form you must inform the ordaining, commissioning, or

(continued on page 2)

Cat. No. 41586H   Form **4361** (Rev. 6-91)

Exhibit 2-2

Form **941**
(Rev. January 1991)
Department of the Treasury
Internal Revenue Service

4141

Employer's Quarterly Federal Tax Return

▶ See Circular E for more information concerning employment tax returns.

Please type or print.

OMB No. 1545-0029
Expires: 5-31-93

Your name, address, employer identification number, and calendar quarter of return. (If not correct, please change.)

Name (as distinguished from trade name)	Date quarter ended
Trade name, if any	Employer identification number
Address and ZIP code	

T
FF
FD
FP
I
T

If address is different from prior return, check here ▶ ☐

IRS Use

1 1 1 1 1 1 1 1 1 1   2   3 3 3 3 3 3   4 4 4
5 5 5   6   7   8 8 8 8 8   9 9 9   10 10 10 10 10 10 10 10 10 10

If you do not have to file returns in the future, check here . . . ▶ ☐   Date final wages paid . . . ▶ _____

If you are a seasonal employer, see **Seasonal employers** on page 2 and check here . ▶ ☐

1a	Number of employees (except household) employed in the pay period that includes March 12th ▶	1a	
b	If you are a subsidiary corporation AND your parent corporation files a consolidated Form 1120, enter parent corporation employer identification number (EIN) . . ▶ | 1b | —		
2	Total wages and tips subject to withholding, plus other compensation . . . . . ▶	2	
3	Total income tax withheld from wages, tips, pensions, annuities, sick pay, gambling, etc. . ▶	3	
4	Adjustment of withheld income tax for preceding quarters of calendar year (see instructions) . ▶	4	
5	Adjusted total of income tax withheld (line 3 as adjusted by line 4—see instructions) . . .	5	
6a	Taxable social security wages (Complete line 7) $ ___ × 12.4% (.124) =	6a	
b	Taxable social security tips $ ___ × 12.4% (.124) =	6b	
7	Taxable Medicare wages and tips $ ___ × 2.9% (.029) =	7	
8	Total social security and Medicare taxes (add lines 6a, 6b, and 7)	8	
9	Adjustment of social security and Medicare taxes (see instructions for required explanation) . .	9	
10	Adjusted total of social security and Medicare taxes (line 8 as adjusted by line 9—see instructions) ▶	10	
11	Backup withholding (see instructions)	11	
12	Adjustment of backup withholding tax for preceding quarters of calendar year.	12	
13	Adjusted total of backup withholding (line 11 as adjusted by line 12)	13	
14	**Total taxes** (add lines 5, 10, and 13)	14	
15	Advance earned income credit (EIC) payments made to employees, if any . . . . . ▶	15	
16	Net taxes (subtract line 15 from line 14). **This should equal line IV below** (plus line IV of Schedule A (Form 941) if you have treated backup withholding as a separate liability)	16	
17	**Total deposits for quarter,** including overpayment applied from a prior quarter, from your records. ▶	17	
18	**Balance due** (subtract line 17 from line 16). This should be less than $500. Pay to IRS. . . ▶	18	
19	**Overpayment,** if line 17 is more than line 16, enter here ▶ $ _____ and check if to be:		

☐ Applied to next return   **OR**   ☐ Refunded.

Record of Federal Tax Liability (You must complete if line 16 is $500 or more and Schedule B is not attached.) See instructions before checking these boxes.
Check only if you made deposits using the 95% rule ▶ ☐   Check only if you are a first time 3-banking-day depositor. . . ▶ ☐

Do NOT Show Federal Tax Deposits Here

Date wages paid	Show tax liability here, **not deposits.** IRS gets deposit data from FTD coupons.		
	First month of quarter	Second month of quarter	Third month of quarter
1st through 3rd	A	I	Q
4th through 7th	B	J	R
8th through 11th	C	K	S
12th through 15th	D	L	T
16th through 19th	E	M	U
20th through 22nd	F	N	V
23rd through 25th	G	O	W
26th through the last	H	P	X
Total liability for month	I	II	III

IV Total for quarter (add lines **I, II,** and **III**). **This should equal line 16 above** . . . . . . ▶

Sign Here

Under penalties of perjury, I declare that I have examined this return, including accompanying schedules and statements, and to the best of my knowledge and belief, it is true, correct, and complete.

Signature ▶ _____   Print Your Name and Title ▶ _____   Date ▶ _____

For Paperwork Reduction Act Notice, see page 2.

Exhibit 2-3

Form **941E**
(Rev. January 1991)
Department of the Treasury
Internal Revenue Service

Quarterly Return of Withheld Federal Income Tax and Medicare Tax

▶ See Circular E for more information concerning Employment Tax Returns

OMB No. 1545-0029
Expires 5-31-93

Your name, address, employer identification number, and calendar quarter of return. (If not correct, please change.)

Name

Date quarter ended

Address and ZIP code

Employer identification number

| T |
| FF |
| FD |
| FP |
| I |
| T |

If address is different from prior return, check here ▶

IRS Use

1 1 1 1 1 1 1 1 1 1   2   3 3 3 3 3 3   4 4 4

5 5 5   6   7   8 8 8 8 8   9 9 9   10 10 10 10 10 10 10 10 10

If you do not have to file returns in the future, check here ▶ ☐   Date final wages paid . . . . . ▶ _____

If you are an intermittent filer, see **Intermittent filers** on page 2 and check here ▶ ☐

Complete for First Quarter Only

1	Number of employees (except household) employed in the pay period that includes March 12th ▶	1	
2	Total wages and tips subject to withholding, plus other compensation . . . . ▶	2	
3	Total income tax withheld from wages, tips, pensions, annuities, sick pay, gambling, etc. . . ▶	3	
4	Adjustment of withheld income tax for preceding quarters of calendar year (see instructions) . ▶	4	
5	Adjusted total of income tax withheld (line 3 as adjusted by line 4)	5	
6	Taxable Medicare wages paid . . . . $ _____ × 2.9% (.029) ▶	6	
7	Adjustment of Medicare tax . . . . ▶	7	
8	Adjusted total of Medicare tax (line 6 as adjusted by line 7).	8	
9	Backup withholding . . . . ▶	9	
10	Adjustment of backup withholding tax for preceding quarters of calendar year . . . . . ▶	10	
11	Adjusted total of backup withholding (line 9 as adjusted by line 10)	11	
12	**Total taxes** (add lines 5, 8, and 11) . . . . ▶	12	
13	Advance earned income credit (EIC) payments paid to employees, if any (see instructions). . . ▶	13	
14	Net taxes (subtract line 13 from line 12). **This should equal line IV below** (plus line IV of Schedule A (Form 941) if you have treated backup withholding as a separate liability)	14	
15	**Total deposits** for quarter, including overpayment applied from prior quarter, from your records . ▶	15	
16	**Balance due** (subtract line 15 from line 14). This should be less than $500. Pay to IRS . . ▶	16	
17	**Overpayment,** if line 15 is more than line 14, enter here ▶ $ _____ and check if to be:		

☐ Applied to next return   OR   ☐ Refunded

Record of Federal Tax Liability (You must complete if line 14 is $500 or more and Schedule B (Form 941) is not required.)
See the instructions before checking these boxes.
Check if you made deposits using the 95% rule ▶ ☐   Check if you are a first time 3-banking-day depositor ▶ ☐

Date wages paid		First month of quarter		Second month of quarter		Third month of quarter
		Show tax liability here, *not* deposits. IRS gets deposit data from FTD coupons.				
1st through 3rd	A		I		Q	
4th through 7th	B		J		R	
8th through 11th	C		K		S	
12th through 15th	D		L		T	
16th through 19th	E		M		U	
20th through 22nd	F		N		V	
23rd through 25th	G		O		W	
26th through the last	H		P		X	
Total liability for month	I		II		III	

(left margin: Do NOT Show Federal Tax Deposits Here)

IV Total for quarter (add lines *I*, *II*, and *III*). This should equal line 14 above . . . . ▶

Sign Here

Under penalties of perjury, I declare that I have examined this return, including accompanying schedules and statements, and to the best of my knowledge and belief, it is true, correct, and complete.

Signature ▶ _____   Print Name and Title ▶ _____   Date ▶ _____

For Paperwork Reduction Act Notice, see page 2.

Form **941E** (Rev. 1-91)

Exhibit 2-4

1991 Form W-4

Purpose. Complete Form W-4 so that your employer can withhold the correct amount of Federal income tax from your pay.

Exemption From Withholding. Read line 6 of the certificate below to see if you can claim exempt status. *If exempt, complete line 6; but do not complete lines 4 and 5.* No Federal income tax will be withheld from your pay. Your exemption is good for one year only. It expires February 15, 1992.

Basic Instructions. Employees who are not exempt should complete the Personal Allowances Worksheet. Additional worksheets are provided on page 2 for employees to adjust their withholding allowances based on itemized deductions, adjustments to income, or two-earner/two-job situations. Complete all worksheets that apply to your situation. The worksheets will help you figure the number of withholding allowances you are entitled to claim. However, you may claim fewer allowances than this.

Head of Household. Generally, you may claim head of household filing status on your tax return only if you are unmarried and pay more than 50% of the costs of keeping up a home for yourself and your dependent(s) or other qualifying individuals.

Nonwage Income. If you have a large amount of nonwage income, such as interest or dividends, you should consider making estimated tax payments using Form 1040-ES. Otherwise, you may find that you owe additional tax at the end of the year.

Two-Earner/Two-Jobs. If you have a working spouse or more than one job, figure the total number of allowances you are entitled to claim on all jobs using worksheets from only one Form W-4. This total should be divided among all jobs. Your withholding will usually be most accurate when all allowances are claimed on the W-4 filed for the highest paying job and zero allowances are claimed for the others.

Advance Earned Income Credit. If you are eligible for this credit, you can receive it added to your paycheck throughout the year. For details, get Form W-5 from your employer.

Check Your Withholding. After your W-4 takes effect, you can use **Pub. 919**, Is My Withholding Correct for 1991?, to see how the dollar amount you are having withheld compares to your estimated total annual tax. Call 1-800-829-3676 to order this publication. Check your local telephone directory for the IRS assistance number if you need further help.

Personal Allowances Worksheet For 1991, the value of your personal exemption(s) is reduced if your income is over $100,000 ($150,000 if married filing jointly, $125,000 if head of household, or $75,000 if married filing separately). Get Pub. 919 for details.

A Enter "1" for **yourself** if no one else can claim you as a dependent . . . . **A** _____

B Enter "1" if:
   1. You are single and have only one job; or
   2. You are married, have only one job, and your spouse does not work; or   . . **B** _____
   3. Your wages from a second job or your spouse's wages (or the total of both) are $1,000 or less.

C Enter "1" for your **spouse**. But, you may choose to enter "0" if you are married and have either a working spouse or more than one job (this may help you avoid having too little tax withheld) . . . . **C** _____

D Enter number of **dependents** (other than your spouse or yourself) whom you will claim on your tax return . . . . . **D** _____

E Enter "1" if you will file as **head of household** on your tax return (see conditions under "Head of Household," above) . . **E** _____

F Enter "1" if you have at least $1,500 of **child or dependent care expenses** for which you plan to claim a credit . . . . **F** _____

G Add lines A through F and enter total here . . . . ▶ **G** _____

For accuracy, do all worksheets that apply.
- If you plan to **itemize or claim adjustments to income** and want to reduce your withholding, see the Deductions and Adjustments Worksheet on page 2.
- If you are **single** and have **more than one job** and your combined earnings from all jobs exceed $27,000 OR if you are **married** and have a **working spouse or more than one job,** and the combined earnings from all jobs exceed $46,000, see the Two-Earner/Two-Job Worksheet on page 2 if you want to avoid having too little tax withheld.
- If **neither** of the above situations applies, **stop here** and enter the number from line G on line 4 of Form W-4 below.

- **Cut here and give the certificate to your employer. Keep the top portion for your records.** -

Form **W-4**
Department of the Treasury
Internal Revenue Service

Employee's Withholding Allowance Certificate
▶ **For Privacy Act and Paperwork Reduction Act Notice, see reverse.**

OMB No. 1545-0010
1991

1 Type or print your first name and middle initial Last name	**2** Your social security number

Home address (number and street or rural route)

City or town, state, and ZIP code

3 Marital status
  ☐ Single   ☐ Married
  ☐ Married, but withhold at higher Single rate.
Note: *If married, but legally separated, or spouse is a nonresident alien, check the Single box.*

4 Total number of allowances you are claiming (from line G above or from the Worksheets on back if they apply) . . . **4** _____

5 Additional amount, if any, you want deducted from each pay . . . . **5** $ _____

6 I claim exemption from withholding and I certify that I meet **ALL** of the following conditions for exemption:
- Last year I had a right to a refund of **ALL** Federal income tax withheld because I had **NO** tax liability; **AND**
- This year I expect a refund of **ALL** Federal income tax withheld because I expect to have **NO** tax liability; **AND**
- This year if my income exceeds $550 and includes nonwage income, another person cannot claim me as a dependent.

If you meet all of the above conditions, enter the year effective and "EXEMPT" here . . . . . ▶ **6** 19____

7 Are you a full-time student? (**Note:** *Full-time students are not automatically exempt.*) . . . . **7** ☐ Yes ☐ No

Under penalties of perjury, I certify that I am entitled to the number of withholding allowances claimed on this certificate or entitled to claim exempt status.

Employee's signature ▶ _____ Date ▶ _____ , 19____

8 Employer's name and address (**Employer:** Complete 8 and 10 **only if sending to IRS**)	**9** Office code (optional)	**10** Employer identification number

Exhibit 2-5

[The IRA/SSA will not accept photocopies of Copy A.—CCH.]

[Copies A—D, 1 and 2 of the original Form W-2 are printed three forms to a unperforated page.—CCH.|

1 Control number	22222	For Official Use Only ▶ OMB No. 1545-0008		

2 Employer's name, address, and ZIP code	6 Statutory employee ☐ Deceased ☐ Pension plan ☐ Legal rep. ☐ 942 emp. ☐ Subtotal ☐ Deferred compensation ☐ Void ☐

	7 Allocated tips	8 Advance EIC payment
	9 Federal income tax withheld	10 Wages, tips, other compensation

3 Employer's identification number	4 Employer's state I.D. number	11 Social security tax withheld	12 Social security wages
5 Employee's social security number		13 Social security tips	14 Medicare wages and tips

19a Employee's name (first, middle, last)	15 Medicare tax withheld	16 Nonqualified plans
	17 See Instrs. for Form W-2	18 Other

19b Employee's address and ZIP code

20	21	22 Dependent care benefits	23 Benefits included in Box 10
24 State income tax	25 State wages, tips, etc.	26 Name of state	27 Local income tax	28 Local wages, tips, etc.	29 Name of locality

Copy A For Social Security Administration   Department of the Treasury—Internal Revenue Service

*Form **W-2 Wage and Tax Statement 1991**

For Paperwork Reduction Act Notice, see separate instructions.

Do NOT Cut or Separate Forms on This Page

19b Employee's address and ZIP code

20	21	22 Dependent care benefits	23 Benefits included in Box 10
24 State income tax	25 State wages, tips, etc.	26 Name of state	27 Local income tax	28 Local wages, tips, etc.	29 Name of locality

Copy A For Social Security Administration   Department of the Treasury—Internal Revenue Service

*Form **W-2 Wage and Tax Statement 1991**

For Paperwork Reduction Act Notice, see separate instructions.

Do NOT Cut or Separate Forms on This Page

19b Employee's address and ZIP code

20	21	22 Dependent care benefits	23 Benefits included in Box 10
24 State income tax	25 State wages, tips, etc.	26 Name of state	27 Local income tax	28 Local wages, tips, etc.	29 Name of locality

Copy A For Social Security Administration   Department of the Treasury—Internal Revenue Service

*Form **W-2 Wage and Tax Statement 1991**

For Paperwork Reduction Act Notice, see separate instructions.

Exhibit 2-6

1 Control number		OMB No. 1545-0008				

	2 941/941E ☐ Military ☐ 943 ☐	3 Employer's state I.D. number	5 Total number of statements
Kind of Payer ►	CT-1 ☐ 942 ☐ Medicare govt. emp. ☐	4	

6 Establishment number	7 Allocated tips	8 Advance EIC payments
9 Federal income tax withheld	10 Wages, tips, and other compensation	11 Social security tax withheld
12 Social security wages	13 Social security tips	14 Medicare wages and tips
15 Medicare tax withheld	16 Nonqualified plans	17 Deferred compensation

18 Employer's identification number	19 Other EIN used this year
20 Employer's name	21 Dependent care benefits

	23 Adjusted total social security wages and tips
YOUR COPY	24 Adjusted total Medicare wages and tips
	25 Income tax withheld by third-party payer
22 Employer's address and ZIP code	

Form **W-3 Transmittal of Income and Tax Statements 1991**   Department of the Treasury Internal Revenue Service

Changes You Should Note

The 1991 Form W-3 has been revised to add new Boxes 14, 15, and 24. Please read the instructions carefully before completing this form.

General Instructions

If you issue multiple Forms W-2 to show state or local tax data, do NOT report the same Federal tax data to the Social Security Administration (SSA) on more than one Copy A.

Employers filing privately printed Forms W-2 must file Forms W-3 that are the same width as Form W-2.

Who Must File.—Employers and other payers must file Form W-3 to send Copy A of Forms W-2.

A transmitter or sender (including a service bureau, paying agent, or disbursing agent) may sign Form W-3 for the employer or payer only if the sender:

(a) Is authorized to sign by an agency agreement (either oral, written, or implied) that is valid under state law; and

(b) Writes "For (name of payer)" next to the signature.

If an authorized sender signs for the payer, the payer is still responsible for filing, when due, a correct and complete Form W-3 and attachments, and is subject to any penalties that result from not complying with these requirements. Be sure the payer's name and employer identification number on Forms W-2 and W-3 are the same as those used on the Form 941, 942, or 943 filed by or for the payer.

If you buy or sell a business during the year, see Rev. Proc. 84-77, 1984-2 C.B. 753, for details on who should file the employment tax returns.

Undeliverable Forms W-2. —Keep for 4 years any employee (recipient) copies of Forms W-2 that you tried to deliver but could not.

Reporting on Magnetic Media.— You must file Forms W-2 with SSA on magnetic media instead of using the paper Copy A of Forms W-2 and Form W-3 if you file **250 or more forms.** You may be charged a penalty if you fail to file on magnetic media when required.

If you are filing Forms W-2 using magnetic media, you may also need **Form 6559**, Transmitter Report of Magnetic Media Filing, and **Form 6560**, Employer Summary of Form W-2 Magnetic Media Wage Information.

You can get magnetic media reporting specifications at most SSA offices. You may also get this information by writing to the Social Security Administration, P.O. Box 2317, Baltimore, MD 21235, Attn: Magnetic Media Coordinator.

When To File.—File Form W-3, with Copy A of Forms W-2, by March 2, 1992. You may be penalized if you do not include the correct information on the return or if you file the return late.

You may request an extension of time to file by sending **Form 8809**, Request for Extension of Time To File Information Returns, to the address shown on that form. You must request the extension before the due date of the returns for your request to be considered. See Form 8809 for more details.

Shipping and Mailing.—If you send more than one type of form, please group forms of the same type and send them in separate groups. See the specific instructions for Box 2, below.

Please do not staple Form W-3 to the related Forms W-2. These forms are machine read, and staple holes or tears cause the machine to jam.

If you have a large number of Forms W-2 to send with one Form W-3, you may send them in separate packages. Show your name and employer identification

number on each package. Number them in order (1 of 4, 2 of 4, etc.) and place Form W-3 in package one. Show the number of packages at the bottom of Form W-3 below the title. If you mail them, you must send them first class.

Specific Instructions

Since the form will be read by optical scanning machines, please type entries if possible. Send the whole first page of Form W-3 with Copy A of Forms W-2. Make all dollar entries without the dollar sign but with the decimal point (000.00).

The following instructions are for boxes on the form. If any entry does not apply to you, leave it blank. (Household employers, see the instructions on Form 942. Third-party payers of sick pay, see *Sick Pay*, later.)

Box 1—Control number.—This is an optional box which you may use for numbering the whole transmittal.

Box 2—Kind of Payer.—Put an X in the checkbox that applies to you. **Check only one box.** If you have more than one type, send each with a separate Form W-3.

941/941E.—Check this box if you file **Form 941**, Employer's Quarterly Federal Tax Return, or **941E**, Quarterly Return of Withheld Federal Income Tax and Hospital Insurance (Medicare) Tax, and none of the other five categories applies.

Military.—Check this box if you are a military employer sending Forms W-2 for members of the uniformed services.

943.—Check this box if you file **Form 943**, Employer's Annual Tax Return for Agricultural Employees, and you are sending forms for agricultural employees. For other employees who are not agricultural employees, send the nonagricultural employees' Forms W-2 with a Form W-3 that generally has a checkmark in the 941/941E box.

Exhibit 2-7

[Caution: The IRS will not accept photocopies of Copy A; see the 1991 instructions for Forms 1099.—CCH.]

[Copies A—C of original Form 1099 are each printed with three forms to an unperforated page.]

9595 ☐ VOID ☐ CORRECTED

Type or machine print PAYER'S name, street address, city, state, and ZIP code		1 Rents $	OMB No. 1545-0115	**Miscellaneous Income**
		2 Royalties $	19**91**	
		3 Prizes, awards, etc. $		
PAYER'S Federal identification number	RECIPIENT'S identification number	4 Federal income tax withheld $	5 Fishing boat proceeds $	**Copy A** For **Internal Revenue Service Center**
Type or machine print RECIPIENT'S name		6 Medical and health care payments $	7 Nonemployee compensation $	**File with Form 1096.**
Street address (including apt. no.)		8 Substitute payments in lieu of dividends or interest $	9 Payer made direct sales of $5,000 or more of consumer products to a buyer (recipient) for resale ▶ ☐	For Paperwork Reduction Act Notice and instructions for completing this
City, state, and ZIP code		10 Crop insurance proceeds $	11 State income tax withheld $	form, see Instructions for Forms 1099, 1098, 5498,
Account number (optional)	2nd TIN Not. ☐	12 State/Payer's state number		and W-2G.

Form **1099-MISC**   **Do NOT Cut or Separate Forms on This Page**   Department of the Treasury - Internal Revenue Service

☐ CORRECTED (if checked)

PAYER'S name, street address, city, state, and ZIP code		1 Rents $	OMB No. 1545-0115	**Miscellaneous Income**
		2 Royalties $	19**91**	
		3 Prizes, awards, etc. $		
PAYER'S Federal identification number	RECIPIENT'S identification number	4 **Federal income tax withheld** $	5 Fishing boat proceeds $	**Copy B For Recipient**
RECIPIENT'S name		6 Medical and health care payments $	7 Nonemployee compensation $	This is important tax information and is being furnished to the Internal Revenue Service. If you are
Street address (including apt. no.)		8 Substitute payments in lieu of dividends or interest $	9 Payer made direct sales of $5,000 or more of consumer products to a buyer (recipient) for resale ▶ ☐	required to file a return, a negligence penalty or other sanction may be imposed on you if this
City, state, and ZIP code		10 Crop insurance proceeds $	11 State income tax withheld $	income is taxable and the IRS determines that it has not been
Account number (optional)		12 State/Payer's state number		reported.

Form **1099-MISC**   Department of the Treasury - Internal Revenue Service

☐ VOID ☐ CORRECTED

PAYER'S name, street address, city, state, and ZIP code		1 Rents $	OMB No. 1545-0115	**Miscellaneous Income**
		2 Royalties $	19**91**	
		3 Prizes, awards, etc. $		
PAYER'S Federal identification number	RECIPIENT'S identification number	4 Federal income tax withheld $	5 Fishing boat proceeds $	**Copy C For Payer**
RECIPIENT'S name		6 Medical and health care payments $	7 Nonemployee compensation $	For Paperwork Reduction Act Notice and
Street address (including apt. no.)		8 Substitute payments in lieu of dividends or interest $	9 Payer made direct sales of $5,000 or more of consumer products to a buyer (recipient) for resale ▶ ☐	instructions for completing this form, see Instructions for
City, state, and ZIP code		10 Crop insurance proceeds $	11 State income tax withheld $	Forms 1099, 1098, 5498, and
Account number (optional)	2nd TIN Not. ☐	12 State/Payer's state number		W-2G.

Form **1099-MISC**   Department of the Treasury - Internal Revenue Service

Exhibit 2-8

[Caution: The IRS will not accept photocopies of Copy A; see the 1991 instructions for Forms 1099.—CCH.]

[Copies A—C of original Form 1099 are each printed with three forms to an unperforated page.]

9292 ☐ VOID ☐ CORRECTED

Type or machine print PAYER'S name, street address, city, state, and ZIP code	Payer's RTN (optional)	OMB No. 1545-0112		
		19**91**	Interest Income	
PAYER'S Federal identification number	RECIPIENT'S identification number	1 Interest income not included in Box 3 $		Copy A
Type or machine print RECIPIENT'S name		2 Early withdrawal penalty $	3 Interest on U.S. Savings Bonds and Treas. obligations $	For **Internal Revenue Service Center** File with Form 1096.
Street address (including apt. no.)		4 Federal income tax withheld $		For Paperwork Reduction Act Notice and
City, state, and ZIP code		5 Foreign tax paid	6 Foreign country or U.S. possession	instructions for completing this form, see
Account number (optional)	2nd TIN Not. ☐	$		Instructions for Forms 1099, 1098, 5498, and W-2G.

* Form **1099-INT**

Department of the Treasury - Internal Revenue Service

Do NOT Cut or Separate Forms on This Page

☐ CORRECTED (if checked)

PAYER'S name, street address, city, state, and ZIP code	Payer's RTN (optional)	OMB No. 1545-0112		
		19**91**	Interest Income	
PAYER'S Federal identification number	RECIPIENT'S identification number	1 Interest income not included in Box 3 $		Copy B For Recipient
RECIPIENT'S name		2 Early withdrawal penalty $	3 Interest on U.S. Savings Bonds and Treas. obligations $	This is important tax information and is being furnished to the Internal Revenue Service. If you are
Street address (including apt. no.)		4 Federal income tax withheld $		required to file a return, a negligence penalty or other
City, state, and ZIP code		5 Foreign tax paid	6 Foreign country or U.S. possession	sanction may be imposed on you if this income is taxable and
Account number (optional)		$		the IRS determines that it has not been reported.

Form **1099-INT**

Department of the Treasury - Internal Revenue Service

☐ VOID ☐ CORRECTED

PAYER'S name, street address, city, state, and ZIP code	Payer's RTN (optional)	OMB No. 1545-0112		
		19**91**	Interest Income	
PAYER'S Federal identification number	RECIPIENT'S identification number	1 Interest income not included in Box 3 $		Copy C For Payer
RECIPIENT'S name		2 Early withdrawal penalty $	3 Interest on U.S. Savings Bonds and Treas. obligations $	For Paperwork Reduction Act Notice and
Street address (including apt. no.)		4 Federal income tax withheld $		instructions for completing this form, see
City, state, and ZIP code		5 Foreign tax paid	6 Foreign country or U.S. possession	Instructions for Forms 1099, 1098, 5498, and W-2G.
Account number (optional)	2nd TIN Not. ☐	$		

Form **1099-INT**

Department of the Treasury - Internal Revenue Service

Exhibit 2-9

DO NOT STAPLE   6969   ☐ CORRECTED

Form **1096**	**Annual Summary and Transmittal of**	OMB No. 1545-0108
Department of the Treasury Internal Revenue Service	**U.S. Information Returns**	19**91**

ATTACH IRS LABEL HERE

┌ Type or machine print FILER'S name (or attach label)   ┐

   Street address (room or suite number)

   City, state, and ZIP code

└   ┘

If you are not using a preprinted label, enter in Box 1 or 2 below the identification number you used as the filer on the information returns being transmitted. Do not fill in both Boxes 1 and 2.	Name of person to contact if IRS needs more information Telephone number ( )	**For Official Use Only** ☐☐☐☐☐☐ ☐☐

1 Employer identification number	2 Social security number	3 Total number of documents	4 Federal income tax withheld $	5 Total amount reported with this Form 1096 $

Check only one box below to indicate the type of form being transmitted.   If this is your FINAL return, check here . . . . ▶ ☐

W-2G 32	1098 81	1099-A 80	1099-B 79	1099-DIV 91	1099-G 86	1099-INT 92	1099-MISC 95	1099-OID 96	1099-PATR 97	1099-R 98	1099-S 75	5498 28
☐	☐	☐	☐	☐	☐	☐	☐	☐	☐	☐	☐	☐

Under penalties of perjury, I declare that I have examined this return and accompanying documents, and, to the best of my knowledge and belief, they are true, correct, and complete.

Signature ▶ ....   Title ▶ ....   Date ▶ ....

Please return this entire page to the Internal Revenue Service. Photocopies are NOT acceptable.

Instructions

Purpose of Form.—Use this form to transmit paper Forms 1099, 1098, 5498, and W-2G to the Internal Revenue Service. DO NOT USE FORM 1096 TO TRANSMIT MAGNETIC MEDIA. See **Form 4804,** Transmittal of Information Returns Reported on Magnetic Media.

Use of Preprinted Label.—If you received a preprinted label from IRS with Package 1099, place the label in the name and address area of this form inside the brackets. Make any necessary changes to your name and address on the label. However, do not use the label if the taxpayer identification number (TIN) shown is incorrect. **Do not prepare your own label. Use only the IRS-prepared label that came with your Package 1099.**

If you are not using a preprinted label, enter the filer's name, address (including room, suite, or other unit number), and TIN in the spaces provided on the form.

Filer.—**The name, address, and TIN of the filer on this form must be the same as those you enter in the upper left area of Form 1099, 1098, 5498, or W-2G.** A filer includes a payer, a recipient of mortgage interest payments, a broker, a barter exchange, a person reporting real estate transactions, a trustee or issuer of an individual retirement arrangement (including an IRA or SEP), and a lender who acquires an interest in secured property or who has reason to know that the property has been abandoned.

Transmitting to IRS.—Group the forms by form number and transmit each group with a **separate** Form 1096. For example, if you must file both Forms 1098 and Forms 1099-A, complete one Form 1096 to transmit your Forms 1098 and another Form 1096 to transmit your Forms 1099-A. Also submit a separate Form 1096 for each type of corrected form.

Box 1 or 2.—Complete only if you are not using a preprinted IRS label. Individuals not in a trade or business must enter their social security number in Box 2; sole proprietors and all others must enter their employer identification number in Box 1. However, sole proprietors who are not required to have an employer identification number must enter their social security number in Box 2.

Box 3.—Enter the number of forms you are transmitting with this Form 1096. Do not include blank or voided forms or the Form 1096 in your total. Enter the number of correctly completed forms, not the number of pages, being transmitted. For example, if you send one page of three-to-a-page Forms 5498 with a Form 1096 and you have correctly completed two Forms 5498 on that page, enter 2 in Box 3 of Form 1096.

Box 4.—Enter the total Federal income tax withheld shown on the forms being transmitted with this Form 1096.

Box 5.—No entry is required if you are filing Form 1099-A or 1099-G. For all other forms, enter the total of the amounts from the specific boxes of the forms listed below:

Form W-2G	Box 1
Form 1098	Boxes 1 and 2
Form 1099-B	Boxes 2 and 3
Form 1099-DIV	Boxes 1a, 5, and 6
Form 1099-INT	Boxes 1 and 3
Form 1099-MISC	Boxes 1, 2, 3, 5, 6, 7, 8, and 10
Form 1099-OID	Boxes 1 and 2
Form 1099-PATR	Boxes 1, 2, 3, and 5
Form 1099-R	Box 1
Form 1099-S	Box 2
Form 5498	Boxes 1 and 2

For Paperwork Reduction Act Notice, see the separate Instructions for Forms 1099, 1098, 5498, and W-2G.   Form **1096** (1991)

Exhibit 2-10

Form **5578**
(Rev. March 1990)
Department of the Treasury
Internal Revenue Service

Annual Certification of Racial Nondiscrimination for a Private School Exempt from Federal Income Tax
(For Use by Organizations That Do Not File Form 990 or 990EZ)

OMB No. 1545-0213
Expires 03-31-93

For IRS use ONLY ▶

For the period beginning _____ , 19 ___ , and ending _____ , 19 ___

1a Name of organization which operates, supervises, and/or controls school(s)

1b Employer identification number

Address (number and street)

City or town, state, and ZIP code

2a Name of central organization holding group exemption letter covering the school(s). (If same as 1a above, write "Same" and complete 2c.) If the organization in 1a above holds an individual exemption letter, write "Not Applicable."

2b Employer identification number

Address (number and street)

2c Group exemption number (see instructions under **Definitions**)

City or town, state, and ZIP code

3a Name of school (if more than one school, write "See Attached," and attach list of the names, addresses, ZIP codes, and employer identification numbers of the schools). If same as 1a above, write "Same."

3b Employer identification number, if any

Address (number and street)

City or town, state, and ZIP code

Under penalties of perjury, I hereby certify that I am authorized to take official action on behalf of the above school(s) and that to the best of my knowledge and belief the school(s) has (have) satisfied the applicable requirements of section 4.01 through 4.05 of Revenue Procedure 75-50 for the period covered by this certification.

_____ (Signature)   _____ (Title or authority of signer)   _____ (Date)

Instructions

This form is open to public inspection.

Paperwork Reduction Act Notice.—We ask for this information to carry out the Internal Revenue laws of the United States. We need it to ensure that taxpayers are complying with these laws. You are required to give us this information.

The time needed to complete and file this form will vary depending on individual circumstances. The estimated average time is 4 hours and 45 minutes. If you have comments concerning the accuracy of this time estimate or suggestions for making this form more simple, we would be happy to hear from you. You can write to the **Internal Revenue Service,** Washington, DC 20224, Attention: IRS Reports Clearance Officer, T:FP; or the **Office of Management and Budget,** Paperwork Reduction Project (1545-0213), Washington, DC 20503.

Purpose of Form

Form 5578 may be used by organizations that operate tax-exempt private schools to provide the Internal Revenue Service with the annual certification of racial nondiscrimination required by Rev. Proc. 75-50, 1975-2 C.B. 587.

Who Must File

Every organization that claims exemption from Federal income tax under section 501(c)(3) of the Internal Revenue Code and that operates, supervises, or controls a private school or schools must file a certification of racial nondiscrimination. If an organization is required to file **Form 990,** Return of Organization Exempt From Income Tax, or **Form 990EZ,** Short Form Return of Organization Exempt From Income Tax, either as a separate return or as part of a group return, the certification must be made on Schedule A (Form 990) rather than on this form.

An authorized official of a central organization may file one form to certify for the school activities of subordinates, that would otherwise be required to file on an individual basis, but only if the central organization has enough control over the schools listed on the form to ensure that the schools maintain a racially nondiscriminatory policy as to students.

Definitions

A **"racially nondiscriminatory policy as to students"** means that the school admits the students of any race to all the rights, privileges, programs, and activities generally accorded or made available to students at that school and that the school does not discriminate on the basis of race in the administration of its educational policies, admissions policies, scholarship and loan programs, and other school-administered programs.

The IRS considers discrimination on the basis of race to include discrimination on the basis of color and national or ethnic origin.

A **school** is an educational organization which normally maintains a regular faculty and curriculum and normally has a regularly enrolled body of pupils or students in attendance at the place where its educational activities are regularly carried on. The term includes primary, secondary, preparatory, or high schools, and colleges and universities, whether operated as a separate legal entity or as an activity of a church or other organization described in Code section 501(c)(3). The term also includes pre-schools and any other organization that is a school as defined in Code section 170(b)(1)(A)(ii).

A **central organization** is an organization which has one or more subordinates under its general supervision or control. A subordinate is a chapter, local, post, or other unit of a central organization. A central organization may also be a subordinate, as in the case of a state organization which has subordinate units and is itself affiliated with a national organization.

The **group exemption number (GEN)** is a four-digit number issued to a central organization by the IRS. It identifies a central organization that has received a ruling from the IRS recognizing on a group basis the exemption from Federal income tax of the central organization and its covered subordinates.

When To File

Under Rev. Proc. 75-50, a certification of racial nondiscrimination must be filed annually by the 15th day of the 5th month following the end of the organization's calendar year or fiscal period.

Where To File

If the principal office of the organization is located in	Use the following Internal Revenue Service Center address
Alabama, Arkansas, Florida, Georgia, Louisiana, Mississippi, North Carolina, South Carolina, Tennessee	Atlanta, GA 39901
Arizona, Colorado, Kansas, New Mexico, Oklahoma, Texas, Utah, Wyoming	Austin, TX 73301
Indiana, Kentucky, Michigan, Ohio, West Virginia	Cincinnati, OH 45999
Alaska, California, Hawaii, Idaho, Nevada, Oregon, Washington	Fresno, CA 93888
Connecticut, Delaware, Maine, Massachusetts, New Hampshire, New Jersey, New York, Pennsylvania (ZIP codes beginning with 169–171 and 173–196 only), Rhode Island, Vermont	Holtsville, NY 00501
Illinois, Iowa, Minnesota, Missouri, Montana, Nebraska, North Dakota, South Dakota, Wisconsin	Kansas City, MO 64999
District of Columbia, Maryland, Pennsylvania (ZIP codes beginning with 150–168 and 172 only), Virginia, any U.S. possession, any foreign country	Philadelphia, PA 19255

Form **5578** (Rev. 3-90)

Exhibit 2-11

Form **8283**
(Rev. March 1990)

Department of the Treasury
Internal Revenue Service

Noncash Charitable Contributions

▶ Attach to your tax return if the total claimed deduction for all
property contributed exceeds $500.
▶ See separate Instructions.

OMB No. 1545-0908
Expires 2-28-93

Attachment
Sequence No. **55**

Name(s) shown on your income tax return	Identification number

Note: *Compute the amount of your contribution deduction before completing Form 8283. (See your tax return instructions.)*

Section A   Include in Section A **only** items (or groups of similar items) for which you claimed a deduction of $5,000 or less per item or group, and certain publicly traded securities (see Instructions).

Part I   Information on Donated Property

1	(a) Name and address of the donee organization	(b) Description of donated property (attach a separate sheet if more space is needed)
A		
B		
C		
D		
E		

Note: *If the amount you claimed as a deduction for the item is $500 or less, you do not have to complete columns (d), (e), and (f).*

	(c) Date of the contribution	(d) Date acquired by donor (mo., yr.)	(e) How acquired by donor	(f) Donor's cost or adjusted basis	(g) Fair market value	(h) Method used to determine the fair market value
A						
B						
C						
D						
E						

Part II   Other Information—If you gave less than an entire interest in property listed in Part I, complete lines 2a–2e. If restrictions were attached to a contribution listed in Part I, complete lines 3a–3c.

2   If less than the entire interest in the property is contributed during the year, complete the following:

a   Enter letter from Part I that identifies the property _____ . (If Part II applies to more than one property, attach a separate statement.)

b   Total amount claimed as a deduction for the property listed in Part I for this tax year _____
for any prior tax year(s) _____

c   Name and address of each organization to which any such contribution was made in a prior year (complete only if different than the donee organization above).

Name of charitable organization (donee)

Address (number and street)

City or town, state, and ZIP code

d   The place where any tangible property is located or kept _____

e   Name of any person, other than the donee organization, having actual possession of the property _____

3   If conditions were attached to any contribution listed in Part I, answer the following questions and attach the required statement (see Instructions):

		Yes	No
a	Is there a restriction, either temporary or permanent, on the donee's right to use or dispose of the donated property?		
b	Did you give to anyone (other than the donee organization or another organization participating with the donee organization in cooperative fundraising) the right to the income from the donated property or to the possession of the property, including the right to vote donated securities, to acquire the property by purchase or otherwise, or to designate the person having such income, possession, or right to acquire?		
c	Is there a restriction limiting the donated property for a particular use?		

For Paperwork Reduction Act Notice, see separate Instructions.

Form **8283** (Rev. 3-90)

Exhibit 2-12

Form **8282**
(Rev. March 1990)
Department of the Treasury
Internal Revenue Service

Donee Information Return

(Sale, Exchange, or Other Disposition of Donated Property)
► See instructions on back.

OMB No. 1545-0908
Expires 2-28-93

Give Copy to Donor

Please Print or Type

Name of charitable organization (donee)	Employer identification number
Address (number and street)	
City or town, state, and ZIP code	

Note: *If you are the original donee, **DO NOT** complete Part II, or column (c) of Part III.*

Part I Information on ORIGINAL DONOR and DONEE YOU GAVE THE PROPERTY TO

1a **Name of the original donor** of (first person to give) the property	**1b** Identification number

Note: *Complete lines 2a–2d only if you gave this property to another charitable organization (successor donee).*

2a **Name of charitable organization**	**2b** Identification number (EIN)
2c Address (number and street)	
2d City or town, state, and ZIP code	

Part II Information on PREVIOUS DONEES—Complete this part only if you were not the first donee to receive the property.

If you were the second donee, leave lines 4a–4d blank. If you were a third or later donee, complete lines 3a–4d. On lines 4a–4d give information on the preceding donee (the one who gave you the gift).

3a **Name of original donee**	**3b** Identification number (EIN)
3c Address (number and street)	
3d City or town, state, and ZIP code	
4a **Name of preceding donee**	**4b** Identification number (EIN)
4c Address (number and street)	
4d City or town, state, and ZIP code	

Part III Information on DONATED PROPERTY

(a) Description of donated property sold, exchanged, or otherwise disposed of (attach a separate sheet if more space is needed)	**(b)** Date you received the item(s)	**(c)** Date the first donee received the item(s) (if you weren't the first)	**(d)** Date item(s) sold, exchanged, or otherwise disposed of	**(e)** Amount received upon disposition

Exhibit 2-13

Form 8300

(Rev. January 1990)

Department of the Treasury
Internal Revenue Service

Report of Cash Payments Over $10,000 Received in a Trade or Business

Failure to file this form or filing a false form may result in imprisonment.

▶ See instructions on back.

Please type or print.

OMB No. 1545-0892

Expires: 10-31-92

1 Check appropriate boxes if: **a** ☐ amends prior report; **b** ☐ suspicious transaction.

Part I   Identity of Individual From Whom the Cash Was Received

2 If more than one individual is involved, see instructions and check here . . . . ▶ ☐

3 Last name	**4** First name	**5** Middle initial	**6** Social security number

7 Address (number and street)	**8** Occupation, profession, or business

9 City	**10** State	**11** ZIP code	**12** Country (if not U.S.)	**13** Date of birth (see instructions)

14 Method used to verify identity: **a** Describe identification ▶ ....

b Issued by   **c** Number

Part II   Person (See Definitions) on Whose Behalf This Transaction Was Conducted

15 If this transaction was conducted on behalf of more than one person, see instructions and check here . . . . ▶ ☐

16 This person is an: ☐ individual or ☐ organization   **17** If funded by another party, see instructions and check here . . ▶ ☐

18 Individual's last name or Organization's name	**19** First name	**20** Middle initial	**21** Social security number

22 Alien identification: **a** Describe identification ▶ ....   Employer identification number

b Issued by   **c** Number

23 Address (number and street)	**24** Occupation, profession, or business

25 City	**26** State	**27** ZIP code	**28** Country (if not U.S.)	**29** Date of birth (see instructions)

Part III   Description of Transaction and Method of Payment

30a ☐ personal property purchased   **d** ☐ business services provided   **g** ☐ exchange of cash

b ☐ real property purchased   **e** ☐ intangible property purchased   **h** ☐ escrow or trust funds

c ☐ personal services provided   **f** ☐ debt obligations paid   **i** ☐ other (specify) ▶

31 Specific description of property or service purchased. Give serial or registration number of car, boat, airplane, etc., address of real estate, etc.

....

32 Total price $ .00 **33** Amount of cash received $ .00 **34** Amount in $100 bills or larger $ .00

35 If part of an installment sale, give information below and check box . . . . ▶ ☐   **36** Date of transaction

a Number of payments _____   **b** Amount of each payment $ _____ .00

c Frequency: ☐ monthly   ☐ other (describe)   **d** Balloon payment (amount) $ .00

37 ☐ Paid with U.S. currency   ☐ Paid with foreign currency (country)   Amount (U.S. dollar equivalent) $ .00

Part IV   Business Reporting This Transaction

38 Name of reporting business	**39** Employer identification number

40 Street address where transaction occurred	Social security number

41 City	**42** State	**43** ZIP code	**44** Nature of your business

45 Under penalties of perjury, I declare that to the best of my knowledge the information I have furnished above is true, correct, and complete.

**Sign
Here**

_____   _____   _____   _____

(Authorized signature–See Instructions)   (Title)   (Date signed)   (Telephone number)

Paperwork Reduction Act Notice.—The requested information is useful in criminal, tax, and regulatory investigations, for instance by directing the Federal Government's attention to unusual or questionable transactions. Trades or businesses are required to provide the information under 26 U.S.C. 6050I.

The time needed to complete this form will vary depending on individual circumstances. The estimated average time is 18 minutes. If you have comments concerning the accuracy of this time estimate or suggestions for making this form more simple, you can write to the **Internal Revenue Service,** Washington, DC 20224, Attention: IRS Reports Clearance Officer T:FP; or the **Office of Management and Budget,** Paperwork Reduction Project (1545-0892), Washington, DC 20503.

Form **8300** (Rev. 1-90)

Exhibit 2-14

Form **W-9**
(Rev. April 1990)
Department of the Treasury
Internal Revenue Service

Request for Taxpayer
Identification Number and Certification

**Give this form
to the requester. Do
NOT send to IRS.**

Name (If joint names, list first and circle the name of the person or entity whose number you enter in Part I below. **See instructions under "Name"** if your name has changed.)

Address (number and street)

City, state, and ZIP code

List account number(s)
here (optional)

Part I Taxpayer Identification Number (TIN)

Enter your taxpayer identification number in
the appropriate box. For individuals and sole
proprietors, this is your social security number.
For other entities, it is your employer
identification number. If you do not have a
number, see *How To Obtain a TIN*, below.

Note: *If the account is in more than one name,
see the chart on page 2 for guidelines on whose
number to enter.*

Social security number

OR

Employer identification number

Part II For Payees Exempt From
Backup Withholding (See
Instructions)

Requester's name and address (optional)

Certification.—Under penalties of perjury, I certify that:

(1) The number shown on this form is my correct taxpayer identification number (or I am waiting for a number to be issued to me), **and**

(2) I am not subject to backup withholding because: **(a)** I am exempt from backup withholding, or **(b)** I have not been notified by the
Internal Revenue Service (IRS) that I am subject to backup withholding as a result of a failure to report all interest or dividends, or **(c)**
the IRS has notified me that I am no longer subject to backup withholding.

Certification Instructions.—You must cross out item (2) above if you have been notified by IRS that you are currently subject to backup
withholding because of underreporting interest or dividends on your tax return. For real estate transactions, item (2) does not apply. For
mortgage interest paid, the acquisition or abandonment of secured property, contributions to an individual retirement arrangement (IRA),
and generally payments other than interest and dividends, you are not required to sign the Certification, but you must provide your correct
TIN. (Also see *Signing the Certification* under *Specific Instructions*, on page 2.)

**Please
Sign
Here**

Signature ▶

Date ▶

Instructions

Exhibit 2-15

EMPLOYMENT ELIGIBILITY VERIFICATION (Form I-9)

1 **EMPLOYEE INFORMATION AND VERIFICATION:** (To be completed and signed by employee.)

Name: (Print or Type) Last	First	Middle	Birth Name
Address: Street Name and Number City		State	ZIP Code
Date of Birth (Month/Day/Year)		Social Security Number	

I attest, under penalty of perjury, that I am (check a box):

☐ 1. A citizen or national of the United States.

☐ 2. An alien lawfully admitted for permanent residence (Alien Number A _____ _____)

☐ 3. An alien authorized by the Immigration and Naturalization Service to work in the United States (Alien Number A _____ .
or Admission Number _____ , expiration of employment authorization, if any _____)

I attest, under penalty of perjury, the documents that I have presented as evidence of identity and employment eligibility are genuine and relate to me. I am aware that federal law provides for imprisonment and/or fine for any false statements or use of false documents in connection with this certificate.

Signature	Date (Month/Day/Year)

PREPARER/TRANSLATOR CERTIFICATION (To be completed if prepared by person other than the employee) I attest, under penalty of perjury, that the above was prepared by me at the request of the named individual and is based on all information of which I have any knowledge

Signature	Name (Print or Type)		
Address (Street Name and Number)	City	State	Zip Code

2 **EMPLOYER REVIEW AND VERIFICATION:** (To be completed and signed by employer.)

Instructions:

Examine one document from List A and check the appropriate box, **OR** examine one document from List B **and** one from List C and check the appropriate boxes. Provide the **Document Identification Number** and **Expiration Date** for the document checked.

List A	List B		List C
Documents that Establish Identity and Employment Eligibility	Documents that Establish Identity	**and**	Documents that Establish Employment Eligibility

List A

☐ 1. United States Passport

☐ 2. Certificate of United States Citizenship

☐ 3. Certificate of Naturalization

☐ 4. Unexpired foreign passport with attached Employment Authorization

☐ 5. Alien Registration Card with photograph

Document Identification

_____

Expiration Date (if any)

_____

List B

☐ 1. A State-issued driver's license or a State-issued I.D. card with a photograph, or information, including name, sex, date of birth, height, weight, and color of eyes.
(Specify State)_____)

☐ 2. U.S. Military Card

☐ 3. Other (Specify document and issuing authority)

_____

Document Identification

_____

Expiration Date (if any)

_____

List C

☐ 1 Original Social Security Number Card (other than a card stating it is not valid for employment)

☐ 2. A birth certificate issued by State, county, or municipal authority bearing a seal or other certification

☐ 3. Unexpired INS Employment Authorization Specify form

_____

Document Identification

_____

Expiration Date (if any)

_____

CERTIFICATION: I attest, under penalty of perjury, that I have examined the documents presented by the above individual, that they appear to be genuine and to relate to the individual named, and that the individual, to the best of my knowledge, is eligible to work in the United States.

Signature	Name (Print or Type)	Title
Employer Name	Address	Date

Form I-9 (05/07/87)
OMB No. 1115-0136

U.S. Department of Justice
Immigration and Naturalization Service

Exhibit 2-16

Return of Organization Exempt From Income Tax

Under section 501(c) of the Internal Revenue Code (except black lung benefit trust or private foundation) or section 4947(a)(1) charitable trust

OMB No. 1545-0047

1990

Department of the Treasury
Internal Revenue Service

Note: You may have to use a copy of this return to satisfy state reporting requirements. See instruction E.

For the calendar year 1990, or fiscal year beginning _____, 1990, and ending _____, 19___

Use IRS label. Other-wise, please print or type.	Name of organization	**A** Employer identification number (see instruction S2)
	Number, street, and room (or P.O. box number) (see instruction S1.)	**B** State registration number (see instruction E)
	City or town, state, and ZIP code	**C** If application for exemption is pending, check here ▶ . . . . ☐

D Check type of organization—Exempt under section ▶ ☐ 501(c) ( ) (insert number), OR ▶ ☐ section 4947(a)(1) charitable trust (see instruction C7 and question 92.)

E Accounting method: ☐ Cash ☐ Accrual ☐ Other (specify) ▶

F Is this a group return (see instruction Q) filed for affiliates?. . . . . ☐ Yes ☐ No

G If either answer in F is "Yes," enter four-digit group exemption number (GEN) ▶

If "Yes," enter the number of affiliates for which this return is filed _____

Is this a separate return filed by a group affiliate? . . . . . . ☐ Yes ☐ No

H Check box if address changed ▶ . . . ☐

I Check here ☐ if your gross receipts are normally not more than $25,000 (see instruction B11). You do not have to file a completed return with IRS; but if you received a Form 990 Package in the mail, you should file a return without financial data (see instruction A5). **Some states require a completed return.**

Note: Form 990EZ may be used by organizations with gross receipts less than $100,000 **and** total assets less than $250,000 at end of year.

Section 501(c)(3) organizations and 4947(a)(1) trusts must also complete and attach Schedule A (Form 990). (See instruction C1.)

Part I — Statement of Revenue, Expenses, and Changes in Net Assets or Fund Balances

Revenue	**1**	Contributions, gifts, grants, and similar amounts received:		
	a	Direct public support	1a	
	b	Indirect public support	1b	
	c	Government grants	1c	
	d	**Total** (add lines 1a through 1c) (attach schedule—see instructions)	1d	
	2	Program service revenue (from Part VII, line 93)	2	
	3	Membership dues and assessments (see instructions)	3	
	4	Interest on savings and temporary cash investments	4	
	5	Dividends and interest from securities.	5	
	6a	Gross rents	6a	
	b	Less: rental expenses	6b	
	c	Net rental income or (loss) (line 6a less line 6b)	6c	
	7	Other investment income (describe ▶)	7	
	8a	Gross amount from sale of assets other than inventory	8a	(A) Securities / (B) Other
	b	Less: cost or other basis and sales expenses	8b	
	c	Gain or (loss) (attach schedule) . . .	8c	
	d	Net gain or (loss) (combine line 8c, column (A) and line 8c, column (B))	8d	
	9	Special fundraising events and activities (attach schedule—see instructions):		
	a	Gross revenue (not including $_____ of contributions reported on line 1a)	9a	
	b	Less: direct expenses	9b	
	c	Net income (line 9a less line 9b)	9c	
	10a	Gross sales less returns and allowances	10a	
	b	Less: cost of goods sold	10b	
	c	Gross profit or (loss) (line 10a less line 10b) (attach schedule)	10c	
	11	Other revenue (from Part VII, line 103)	11	
	12	**Total revenue** (add lines 1d, 2, 3, 4, 5, 6c, 7, 8d, 9c, 10c, and 11)	12	
Expenses	**13**	Program services (from line 44, column (B)) (see instructions)	13	
	14	Management and general (from line 44, column (C)) (see instructions)	14	
	15	Fundraising (from line 44, column (D)) (see instructions)	15	
	16	Payments to affiliates (attach schedule—see instructions)	16	
	17	**Total expenses** (add lines 16 and 44, column (A)).	17	
Net Assets	**18**	Excess or (deficit) for the year (subtract line 17 from line 12)	18	
	19	Net assets or fund balances at beginning of year (from line 74, column (A)) . . .	19	
	20	Other changes in net assets or fund balances (attach explanation)	20	
	21	Net assets or fund balances at end of year (combine lines 18, 19, and 20)	21	

For Paperwork Reduction Act Notice, see page 1 of the separate **instructions.**

Form **990** (1990)

Exhibit 2-17

Form **990-T**

Department of the Treasury
Internal Revenue Service

Exempt Organization Business Income Tax Return

For calendar year 1990 or other tax year beginning ....,1990, and ending ....,19.....

▶ For Paperwork Reduction Act Notice, see page 1 of separate Instructions.

OMB No. 1545-0687

1990

Please Print or Type	Name of organization	**A** Employer identification number (Employees' trust, see Instructions for Block A)
	Number, street, and room or suite no. (If a P.O. box, see page 3 of Instructions.)	
	City or town, state, and ZIP code	**B** Unrelated business activity codes (See last page of the Instructions.)

C Check box if address changed . . . . . . ▶ ☐   **D** Exempt under section ▶ ☐ 501( ) ( ) OR ▶ ☐ 408(e)

E Check type of organization . . . . ▶ ☐ Corporation ☐ Trust ☐ Section 401(a) trust ☐ Section 408(a) trust

F Group exemption number (see Instructions for Block F) ▶

▶ **If the unrelated trade or business gross income is $10,000 or less, complete only page 1 and Part III on page 2, and sign the return.**

▶ **If the unrelated trade or business gross income is over $10,000, complete all applicable parts of the form (except lines 1 through 4 on page 1).**

Taxable Income

1	Unrelated trade or business gross income (see Instructions) (state sources ▶ _____)	1
2	Deductions (including net operating loss) (see Instructions)	2
3	Unrelated business taxable income before Specific deduction (line 1 less line 2)	3
4	Specific deduction (see Instructions)	4
5	Unrelated business taxable income (line 3 less line 4 or enter amount from line 33, page 2. If line 4 is greater than line 3, enter the lesser of zero or line 3.)	5

Tax Computation

Organizations Taxable as Corporations (see Instructions for tax computation)

6 Controlled group members (sections 1561 and 1563)—Check here: ☐ and:

  a Enter your share of the $50,000 and $25,000 taxable income bracket amounts (in that order):

   (i) $ _____   (ii) $ _____

  b Enter your share of the additional 5% tax (not to exceed $11,750) $ _____

| 7 | Income tax . . . . | 7 |

Trusts Taxable at Trust Rates (see Instructions for tax computation)

| 8 | Income tax on the amount on line 5 . . . . | 8 |

All Organizations (see Instructions)

9a	Foreign tax credit (corporations attach Form 1118; trusts attach Form 1116)	9a	
b	Other credits (see Instructions)	9b	
c	General business credit.—Check if from: ☐ Form 3800 ☐ Form 3468 ☐ Form 6478 ☐ Form 6765 ☐ Form 8586	9c	
d	Credit for prior year minimum tax (attach Form 8801)	9d	

Tax and Payments

10	Total (add lines 9a through 9d).	10
11	Subtract line 10 from line 7 or line 8	11
12	Recapture taxes. Check if from: ☐ Form 4255 ☐ Form 8611	12
13a	Alternative minimum tax _____ **b** Environmental tax _____	13c
14	**Total tax** (add lines 11, 12, and 13c)	14
15	**Payments: a** 1989 overpayment credited to 1990	15a
b	1990 estimated tax payments	15b
c	Subtotal (add lines 15a and 15b)	15c
d	Tax deposited with Form 7004 or Form 2758	15d
e	Foreign organizations—Tax paid or withheld at source (see Instructions)	15e
f	Other credits and payments (see Instructions)	15f
16	Total credits and payments (add lines 15c through 15f)	16
17	Enter any **penalty** for underpayment of estimated tax. Check ▶ ☐ if Form 2220 is attached . .	17
18	**Tax due**—If the total of lines 14 and 17 is larger than line 16, enter amount owed . . . . . ▶	18
19	**Overpayment**—If line 16 is larger than the total of lines 14 and 17, enter amount overpaid . . ▶	19
20	Enter the amount of line 19 you want: **Credited to 1991 estimated tax** ▶ _____ **Refunded** ▶	20

Please Sign Here

Under penalties of perjury, I declare that I have examined this return, including accompanying schedules and statements, and to the best of my knowledge and belief, it is true, correct, and complete. Declaration of preparer (other than taxpayer) is based on all information of which preparer has any knowledge.

▶ _____ Signature of officer or fiduciary   Date   ▶ _____ Title

Paid Preparer's Use Only	Preparer's signature ▶	Date	Check if self-employed ▶ ☐	Preparer's social security number
	Firm's name (or yours, if self-employed) and address ▶		E.I. No. ▶	
			ZIP code ▶	

Form **990-T** (1990)

Exhibit 2-18

Form 1040-ES | **1991 Payment– Voucher 1**

Department of the Treasury
Internal Revenue Service

OMB No. 1545-0087

Return this voucher with check or money order payable to the **"Internal Revenue Service."** Please write your social security number and "1991 Form 1040-ES" on your check or money order. Please do not send cash. Enclose, but do not staple or attach, your payment with this voucher. File only if you are making a payment of estimated tax.

(Calendar year—Due April 15, 1991)

Amount of payment	Please type or print	Your first name and initial	Your last name	Your social security number
		(If joint payment, complete for spouse)		
		Spouse's first name and initial	Spouse's last name	Spouse's social security number
		Address (number, street, and apt. no.)		
$		City, state, and ZIP code		

Form 1040-ES | **1991 Payment– Voucher 2**

Department of the Treasury
Internal Revenue Service

OMB No. 1545-0087

Return this voucher with check or money order payable to the **"Internal Revenue Service."** Please write your social security number and "1991 Form 1040-ES" on your check or money order. Please do not send cash. Enclose, but do not staple or attach, your payment with this voucher. File only if you are making a payment of estimated tax.

(Calendar year—Due June 17, 1991)

Amount of payment	Please type or print	Your first name and initial	Your last name	Your social security number
		(If joint payment, complete for spouse)		
		Spouse's first name and initial	Spouse's last name	Spouse's social security number
		Address (number, street, and apt. no.)		
$		City, state, and ZIP code		

Form 1040-ES | **1991 Payment– Voucher 3**

Department of the Treasury
Internal Revenue Service

OMB No. 1545-0087

Return this voucher with check or money order payable to the **"Internal Revenue Service."** Please write your social security number and "1991 Form 1040-ES" on your check or money order. Please do not send cash. Enclose, but do not staple or attach, your payment with this voucher. File only if you are making a payment of estimated tax.

(Calendar year—Due Sept 16, 1991)

Amount of payment	Please type or print	Your first name and initial	Your last name	Your social security number
		(If joint payment, complete for spouse)		
		Spouse's first name and initial	Spouse's last name	Spouse's social security number
		Address (number, street, and apt. no.)		
$		City, state, and ZIP code		

Form 1040-ES | **1991 Payment– Voucher 4**

Department of the Treasury
Internal Revenue Service

OMB No. 1545-0087

Return this voucher with check or money order payable to the **"Internal Revenue Service."** Please write your social security number and "1991 Form 1040-ES" on your check or money order. Please do not send cash. Enclose, but do not staple or attach, your payment with this voucher. File only if you are making a payment of estimated tax.

(Calendar year—Due Jan. 15, 1992)

Amount of payment	Please type or print	Your first name and initial	Your last name	Your social security number
		(If joint payment, complete for spouse)		
		Spouse's first name and initial	Spouse's last name	Spouse's social security number
		Address (number, street, and apt. no.)		
$		City, state, and ZIP code		

For Paperwork Reduction Act Notice, see instructions on page 1.　　　　　Page 5

Exhibit 2-19

Introduction to Church Finances

The headlines in the *Los Angeles Times* read "Popular Preacher Finds Himself Beset by Probes of Fraud." A few years earlier, an article in the *Wall Street Journal* was entitled "Church Bonds Plunge into Default." "Church Official Gets Five Years in Tax Scheme" was reported in another large-city newspaper.

Today's church often makes headlines for the wrong reasons. Public details of financial misdeeds by pastors and church boards are becoming all too common. "Forgive us our debts" has taken on a new sense of urgency in recent years. References to "Chapter XI" are being heard in board meetings more frequently. Unfortunately, the context has nothing to do with a reference in the Bible.[5]

The term *stewardship* today has come to represent financial obligation on the part of the donor. Usually the intent of the word is directed toward a congregation, reminding them of their responsibility as it relates to their giving. As the dictionary defines the term, however, a *steward* is "one who manages another's property or financial affairs." It can be illustrated by the role a bank plays. A bank is responsible for other people's money and is expected to provide protection as well as a reasonable return on the investment. In the context of the local church, its pastor and leaders also have a duty to properly manage the funds placed in their care.

As is the case with any other business organization, the complexity of a church's financial procedures is generally directly related to its size. A system that would be adequate for a church with a membership of fifty or sixty will probably not be adequate for one with a membership of five or six hundred. Although the complexity changes with size, the basic objectives of any accounting system remain basically the same.

5. Chapter XI is a part of the Federal Bankruptcy Code and provides a means whereby a financially distressed business may restructure its finances and continue its operation for a period of time.

Objectives of a Church Accounting System

The primary objectives of a church accounting system are generally as follows.

1. The proper protection of cash and other assets

Protection of assets is a basic objective of all accounting systems. Since funds contributed to a church no longer belong to the individual but to the Lord, even greater care should be exercised than what a businessman would exercise in his business. The systems and procedures outlined in this book are designed to help insure the safe handling of funds.

2. Use of funds for the purpose for which they were contributed

If the church accepts gifts designated for a particular purpose that falls outside the church budget, the donors must be assured that the funds will be used in accordance with their wishes. (This issue will be covered more fully in Section 10.)

An essential element of a church accounting system is that it provides an accurate record of individual giving. Since contributions to a church are permitted as an itemized deduction for federal and state income tax purposes, church officers may be called upon to verify contributions that have been claimed as a deduction by members or friends of the church. The availability of accurate information to provide appropriate substantiation to government agencies is therefore important.

Also, an accurate historical record of income and expenses is necessary to properly review past periods and make comparisons with current periods. A comparison of cash income and expense summaries for past periods can be helpful in budget preparation and future planning. This information may also provide insight as to God's direction in a particular area, such as a new building program.

Meeting the Objectives

This section is intended to provide guidance to leaders of local churches as they deal with the financial aspects of church administration. The content of the material presented is hopefully stated in such a manner as to provide sufficient detail so that even those with little or no accounting experience will find it useful. The suggested procedures and forms have been designed so that only a minimum of accounting knowledge is required.[6]

6. Acknowledgment to Paul Stolz, *Manual of Church Financial Procedures* (n.p., 1969).

Because of the differences in size and organizational structure of churches, a variety of different financial and accounting methods are being used by churches today. The objectives of a good accounting system, however, can usually be achieved without the need to change the church's organizational structure. The approach of this section is to speak in general terms so that the objectives can be met within the framework of the existing organizational structure.

The Right Standards

In recent years, concerns have been raised over the ethics and legality of the methods some churches use in the handling of funds. Some of these center on the following areas:

- The improper use of designated gifts
- Property tax exemptions when facilities are used for other than church activities
- The selling of unregistered securities
- Diversion of church donations to private use
- Unreasonable benefits or prerequisites being taken by members of the clergy
- The operation of profit-making business activities
- Questionable business activities
- Unfair treatment of employees

Several years ago, a group of concerned financial officers from both church and para-church organizations had the foresight to recognize the coming danger. Sloppy bookkeeping, unethical fund raising techniques, and the misappropriation of donated monies raised many questions in their minds. In 1979, the Evangelical Council of Financial Accountability (ECFA) was formed for the purpose of establishing basic standards of financial accountability for Christian organizations. To date, the ECFA has been quite effective in its role of promoting professional standards of financial responsibility.

The Right Perspective

Those individuals who must deal with the financial aspects of managing a church have a duty both to their congregations and to the Lord. The responsibility is one of a fiduciary—that is, one who is charged with a confidence or trust as it relates to the management of someone else's money. In fact, the Bible exhortation is clear when it says, "for we have regard for what is honorable, not only in the sight of the Lord, but also in the sight of men" (2 Corinthians 8:21).

The Right People

It is extremely important, therefore, that those individuals who are charged with the oversight of the financial resources of a church be of the highest caliber. You would think that a policy such as this would be a foregone conclusion, especially in a church.

Unfortunately, that isn't always the case. Repeatedly, situations have come up where financial officers were selected simply because they were "good with money." Perhaps the man is a successful businessman, has the largest farm in the community, or, worst of all, is the biggest contributor. If these are the only prerequisites to being the church financial officer, you are flirting with potential problems.

Who *should* serve then? Those men and women who have demonstrated their faithfulness to previously assigned tasks and who evidence the biblical character qualities outlined later in this section.

To develop and carry out a good accounting system, it is helpful for certain individuals and committees to be involved. The titles given to these committees and positions may vary from church to church; however, the titles are not that important. The key is the role they fill in carrying out this vital function.

There may be an overlap between the duties of these committees even to the extent that one committee may perform the function of all groups listed. This would be controlled to some extent by the size of the church. It is absolutely essential, however, that the individual offices listed below be maintained as separate offices. To combine the positions of treasurer and financial secretary, for example, is to destroy the basic concept of internal control necessary for a good accounting system. (The discussion on Internal Control in this section will be explained more fully.) Therefore, these positions should be kept separate even in the smallest church.

The following is a list of the officers and committees:

- *Treasurer*: This officer is entrusted with the receipt, care, and disbursement of funds.
- *Financial Secretary*: This is an individual who receives the church offering envelopes, special offering envelopes, receipts and other evidences of money received, and summary of receipts from money counters for posting to individual member's records.
- *Finance Committee*: A committee usually consisting of three to five members, including the treasurer and financial secretary, it has the responsibility for overseeing the fiscal affairs of the church.
- *Budget Committee*: An ad hoc, or temporary, committee, this group may be composed of the members of the finance committee or it may be expanded to include others. This committee is responsible for preparation of the annual church budget. In a larger church, that would include assembling the budget requests of various boards or departments for inclusion into an overall church budget plan.
- *Counting Committee*: For a larger church, it might be advisable to form a counting committee. This committee may be composed of some of the members of the finance committee and may also include others. It is their responsibility to receive, count, and deposit church funds.

- *Audit Committee*: In a very large church an audit committee would be useful. It should be composed of at least three members. These people may be from the finance committee, be trustees of the church, or be separately appointed or elected. It is the duty of this committee to oversee the audit of the financial records of the church annually or as instructed by the church. If the church is too small for an audit committee, then the ruling board could appoint one or two people who are not on any of the financial groups to review the records.

The financial officers of the church don't necessarily need to be accountants or CPAs. The most practical and effective minimum standard for a financial steward (that is, a money counter, bookkeeper, financial secretary, or treasurer) should be that of being a deacon or wife of a deacon. The qualifications are outlined clearly for us in 1 Timothy 3:8-13 and Titus 1:6-9. Ideally, you would want your highest offices filled by people qualified as—to use New Testament terminology—elders, deacons, or wives of deacons. Starting with the requirements of an elder, or overseer, and moving on through those of a deacon, we find a common thread, a continuous theme—trustworthiness.

- Above reproach—a good reputation in and outside the church (1 Timothy 3:2)
- Temperate—does things in moderation (1 Timothy 3:2)
- Prudent—is shrewd (in a good sense), cautious, and thrifty (1 Timothy 3:2)
- Respectable—one who is deserving of high regard (1 Timothy 3:2)
- Free from the love of money—the pursuit of money does not become a preoccupation (1 Timothy 3:3)
- Manages his own household well—refers to both people and resources (1 Timothy 3:4, 12)

Titus 1:7 sums it up: "The overseer must be above reproach as God's steward." A person can't help but include the word *integrity* in describing this faithful servant. Integrity has been defined as "doing what you're supposed to do when no one is looking." The risk factor in selecting those individuals who are charged with the handling of funds can be greatly reduced when they are chosen on the basis of their character traits first instead of by their secular abilities.

The point is simple: if a person evidences biblical maturity, the likelihood of securing the services of an honest individual are greatly enhanced. If, on the other hand, officers are chosen primarily on the basis of professional prowess, the potential for future problems is increased.

Good people are an essential ingredient to the success of good policies.

Internal Control

A pastor once told me, "I just don't understand all that financial stuff, so I have one of my deacons take care of it!" If your church is small, perhaps your money handling and bookkeeping procedures are quite simple and you feel comfortable with a volunteer handling the load. And that's fine—to a point. However, in order for a medium- to large-size church to function properly today—with the heightened demands for security, the need to protect the church's tax exemption, and the obligation to act responsibly with God's money—some formal system and procedures are a must.

Although it may sound rather technical, the major purposes of sound financial policies and procedures are as follows:

1. To monitor the performance of those charged with the management of funds
2. To provide clear and accurate information to donors and church leadership
3. To protect the assets of the organization

Internal control, as defined in this section, is "the coordination of methods and measures adopted by an organization to check the accuracy and validity of data and to safeguard assets."[7]

When a proper system of internal control is in place, more than one person will be involved in almost all transactions, especially those relating to cash. This provides a natural check of one against the other, which should not be viewed as distrust but merely a form of protection and accountability. It is essential that a church maintain good internal control in not just cash procedures but in all the other accounting areas as well.

Checkpoints

Aside from the obvious requirement to ensure the public that the ministry is not being defrauded, the people who actually handle funds need to be protected from outside charges of wrongdoing. To do this, there should be established cash flow "checkpoints," that is, an internal system of accountability.

Within a church context, there is a general path or route funds travel as they move from the collection plate (receipts) to the process of paying the bills (disbursements). In most smaller churches, one person (usually the bookkeeper or treasurer) oversees all these functions. No matter how small this congregation may be, however, this area should really be given a closer look. If necessary, a flow chart of the path of money through the church can help to identify potential improvements or weaknesses in the system.

The Collection

The handling of cash itself does not result in a permanent, written record until the funds are deposited into the bank. Most other components of the church accounting

---

7. Jerry Rosenberg, *Dictionary of Business and Management* (New York: John Wiler, 1978), p. 231.

system will produce written records as natural by-products. For example, a cash disbursement in the form of a check will produce canceled checks and a bank statement that can be reviewed at a later date. Therefore, the establishment of a good procedure for the handling of cash may be more important than any other area.

The first checkpoint is actually made up of two functions: receiving the collection and counting the money. For the protection of the ushers who receive the money, a certain degree of caution must be exercised, particularly if the offerings are large or the location of the church presents a high degree of risk from theft. If the men must carry the plates outside the auditorium itself, they should proceed in groups of no less than two but not all together as a single group. At no time should a single person be alone with one or more of the collection plates until such time as the funds are physically deposited in a secure place. This will help ensure maximum security of the money and protection for the ushers and will indicate to everyone the importance you place on the proper handling of the Lord's money.

Next, the money should be counted as soon after the collection is taken as practical. This should be done in a secure location, away from public view.

To protect the counters from outside comments or unnecessary problems, it is often a good idea to have these individuals serve on a rotating basis. This helps to protect the confidentiality of members' financial affairs and reduce knowledge of giving patterns.

Another reason for alternating counters is the need to prevent the same people from missing worship services every Sunday. A policy of rotation helps prevent this potential tragedy.

Offering envelopes should be opened individually and checked to determine if the amount on the outside is the same as the amount of money contained within the envelope. Or, if no amount is indicated on the envelope, the proper amount can be filled in. If the contributions are broken down into several funds, envelopes should be used with space provided on the front to enter the amount applicable to each fund. (See Exhibit 3-1.)

After the counting is completed, a summary report should be prepared for accounting purposes. A preprinted form, such as illustrated in Exhibit 3-2, can be especially helpful for this purpose.

Many times an envelope is received without any designation on it or without the donor's wishes being clearly indicated. The finance committee should establish a policy as to how to distribute such gifts. This policy should be approved by the church so that the individuals making contributions will be aware of it.

After the cash has been counted and reconciled, the "flow of funds" is continued to the actual depositing of the money. In some churches this function is performed solely by the treasurer. It is preferable, however, to have the counting committee prepare the actual deposit slip. The treasurer can still deposit the money even if the counting committee prepares the deposit slip.

Again, this procedure needs to be kept simple but secure. Try not to store funds on church premises overnight unless you have a good, fireproof safe. A floor safe is preferable so that it cannot be carted away, and it is essential that the combination be known only by two or three individuals. Police officers tell me churches are "easy pickin's" for even amateur burglars. Security is often inadequate, and money is usually kept locked in desk drawers or file cabinets.

Although most churches have a safe with a combination lock available for temporary storage of cash, if no safe is available, the money could be counted during or immediately following the service and deposited the same day. Another good procedure is to put all the money, uncounted, in a bag and deposit it in the bank night deposit slot during the service. On Monday morning a counting team can go to the bank and count it. This avoids the need to store large sums of money on the church premises overnight or to reveal the combination of the church safe to a number of individuals.

Each time a different person is selected to a position that allows them to know the combination of the safe, the combination should be changed. If this procedure is not followed, in time there will be many people with no accountability who know the combination.

Some churches also carry insurance against theft of funds. Many times, however, these policies state that the insurance does not apply until the offering has been counted. Insurance policies should be examined for these provisions and every effort made to minimize the time interval between receiving an offering and counting it.

If money is deposited in a locked night bank depository, two men should accompany the funds to the bank; however, they should not travel together in the same car. Why? Once more, accountability and safety is the goal. (Detectives with the Los Angeles Police Department have suggested that churches use the two-car procedure.)

Since the morning services usually account for the largest offering, another alternative is to take Sunday morning's offerings to the bank immediately. Then the Sunday evening offering (which is generally much smaller) could either be deposited that night or stored in a safe location until Monday. The chance of theft is greater in the dark, so the key here is to get the largest portion of the cash to the bank as soon as possible.

Disbursements—Check and Double Check

Now that the money is safely tucked away in the bank, we move on to the next "checkpoint"—disbursements. Ideally, this area of internal control encompasses three procedures:

1. The same person who approves purchases should not prepare the checks for payment.
2. The individual who prepares the checks ideally should not be in a position to sign them.
3. The check signer should not complete the circle by also approving the invoices for payment.

The customary "trail" looks something like this:

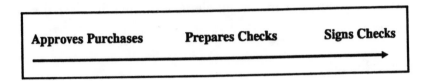

Good internal control would require a break in the direct line:

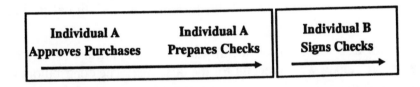

Different individuals can perform each step. The minimum standard would be to place a checkpoint between the function of preparing and signing checks.

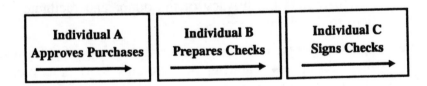

In many small churches, all of these procedures may be performed by the same individual. Nevertheless, it is still preferable to have one of the functions handled by a second person.

A final checkpoint is to place a limit on the amount on which any one individual may draw a check (e.g., $250, $500). This amount should be determined at your ruling board's discretion and be based on the size and number of checks involved. Another means of limiting exposure in this area is to imprint your checks with "two signatures required for checks over $XXX" for maximum protection, $XXX standing for a stipulated amount.

Recording Gifts

Most of the church's income is received through collection plates, and usually more than one person handles the funds. Since all money counters are human (robots haven't taken over this job—yet!), mistakes and temptations will be ever present. If the qualifications for financial stewards are set high enough, however, integrity and honesty will be an inherent part of the job description for this position.

The counting and depositing of funds was discussed previously. At this point, however, I'd like to move to another important element of church internal control: the record of individual giving.

The Envelope, Please!

Most churches use some form of preprinted envelope for offering purposes, though there are still some churches that resist such a system. An envelope system is essential both to developing a good internal cash control system and to contributing to sound accounting procedures. An envelope system produces an individual giving record for both the donor and the church.

In the business world, a record of financial transactions is almost always accompanied by an internal record, along with a receipt for the customer. The contributors to the church financial program likewise should receive some sort of verification of their gift.

The most common envelope system consists of fifty-two numbered envelopes to correspond with each week of the year. These envelopes may also bear a number previously assigned to the donor, and dates for each Sunday of the year. A system using assigned donor numbers serves to protect the privacy of the donor and facilitates the proper posting of contributions to the church records.

Many envelope companies also provide special offering envelopes for Easter, Thanksgiving, and Christmas. Envelopes featuring the church's logo or a picture of the church, Bible verses, or the church's motto may be easily obtained from your local church supply store or denominational headquarters.

Advantages of the Envelope System

In addition to the businesslike way of managing contributions, an envelope system also encourages systematic giving by providing an envelope for each week. The empty envelope is a reminder of the individual's responsibility toward systematic giving.

A complete envelope system will also provide givers with a periodic (quarterly) record of their gifts. The least the church should provide is a record of total contributions at the end of the year. If the donor notes a discrepancy between the summary and his own records, this difference should be called to the attention of the appointed financial officer, thus another cross-check.

Another added advantage of the envelope system is the fact that proper receipts and records are available for the donor to substantiate his claim for income tax deductions. Even though the Internal Revenue Service is relying more on canceled checks now as proof of a donation, they will accept church records as substantiation for gifts of cash.

Unfortunately, many people tend to give only when they are moved emotionally to do so. Don't misunderstand me—the Bible is clear on the fact that we are to give with some emotional attachment. 2 Corinthians 9:7 tells us, "Let each one do just as he has purposed in his heart; not grudgingly or under compulsion; for God loves a cheerful giver." This verse teaches that giving is to be both purposeful (with forethought) and "cheerful." There is certainly room for both emotion and budgeting in giving. The point is, the use of envelopes presupposes some prior thought and preparation for stewardship participation. It also promotes regularity in giving and sets a good example for children.

A final advantage is that all gifts in an envelope appear alike when they are given. Whether it be a large donation or the "widow's mite," it all looks the same. It's the giver's heart that is different!

Keeping the Books

Though this section is designed to keep financial procedures simple, the following discussion may get a little complicated for the untrained person. Therefore, I'll attempt to stay with the basics.

Cash Receipts Journal

Assuming that cash has been properly counted and deposited, a record of the activity should be noted in a cash receipts journal. (See Exhibit 3-3.) By definition, a journal is a chronological record of original entry; it's the "front door" of a formal accounting system. Perhaps you've heard the term *ledger* used at one time or another. A ledger is a record of final entry—no more entries are put into the bookkeeping system after the ledger entry (more about that later).

The cash receipts journal should be maintained by the treasurer or another appropriate person and the format may vary considerably from church to church. What is important is that the journal be designed to meet the specific needs and situation of the church where it is being used. The point is—you need to have one.

The format of the receipts journal depends on the kind of budget used by the church. Generally, there are two basic types: the traditional "fund" budget and the unified budget. The *fund budget* is one where monies are collected and placed in various designated funds or accounts to be disbursed for specific purposes—funds for missions, building projects, debt retirement, or any number of special areas of interest. (A General Fund is usually one of those funds as well.)

The *unified budget*, on the other hand, receives all income into one fund. Then all expenses are paid out of that one fund. Even with the unified budget format, however, it isn't uncommon to have a separate Building Fund because those gifts are often held in reserve for future building-related purposes.

Both budgeting methods require an understanding of the implications and the philosophy behind them and should receive full governing board approval before making changes from one to the other.

A church with a unified budget will require a very simple cash receipts journal since practically no separation of receipts is necessary. In this situation, there will be one column for the cash deposited and another column for the offerings received. It would also be advisable to have a miscellaneous column to be used for unusual items not a part of the regular budget.

The cash receipts journal shown in Exhibit 3-3 is an example of what would be used by a church that is *not* on a unified budget. The column headings should be titled to match the budget categories of the individual church for which it is to be used. Essentially, it should contain one column for the total cash deposited and separate columns for each of the funds maintained by the church. Again, a miscellaneous column is included for special gifts and offerings not included in the regular, established funds.

The Procedure for Maintaining the Journal

1. The treasurer receives the duplicate of the bank deposit slip, plus one copy of the summary of receipts (Exhibit 3-1) from the counting committee.
2. From this slip he completes the "journalizing," that is the entering of the cash received into the journal. This should be done by entering the total cash deposited in the debit "cash deposited" column and the details in those columns where they belong. The loose offering normally would be credited to the General Fund unless there is some other policy established for distributing it. At the end of the month the columns are added to provide the totals for the receipts in each of the funds and the total cash deposited. After these totals have been determined, the sums should be cross-checked by adding up all the credits to make certain they are equal to the debit total in the "cash deposited" column.

Paying the Bills

Up to this point, we have dealt with the different aspects of the receiving and handling of funds. To be consistent with our goal of keeping the "mysteries" of accounting simple, I will continue to offer suggestions that lend themselves to the smaller church.

A brief discussion of a more complex accounting method—Double Entry Book-keeping—will be dealt with later.

Continuing with our policy of maintaining good internal control, as far as possible all disbursements should be made by check. If a Petty Cash Fund is used, it should be reimbursed at least monthly by issuing a check for the exact amount of the expenditures made from it. Receipts and other supporting data should be submitted to the treasurer at the time of reimbursing Petty Cash in the same manner as would be provided for paying any other bill.

The purpose of having cash on hand (hopefully in a locked box) is to pay for those expenses that are small and immediate. This avoids the time and expense required to process a check for inconsequential items.

The matter of cosigning checks has been discussed previously. Normally, only one signature is required on a check for smaller amounts. The cosigner for larger checks should be the treasurer or some other responsible person who is in an accountable position in the financial stream of the organization. An additional signatory allows checks to be written if the treasurer is out of town or is otherwise unavailable.

In some churches, two signatures are required on each and every check, no matter what the amount may be. While this provides a strong checkpoint of accountability, it can be cumbersome for the treasurer who is usually a lay person and not always readily available.

The middle ground in this area would be to have a policy stating that all checks in excess of a particular amount be countersigned. The checks should be made out completely by the treasurer and signed by him prior to being submitted to the second party for the additional signature. Under no circumstances should blank checks be pre-signed.

Check Registers

Many forms of check registers (disbursement journals) are readily available and can be adapted to the needs of the local church. Deposits should be entered in the check register as well as in the cash receipts journal if you wish to maintain a running cash balance of the total in the bank account. Checks written for the payment of bills are entered in the columns provided and distributed to the column headed with the proper expenditure group. Column headings are normally used to separate items into groupings, such as those illustrated below. The correct account number (or account name) is assigned to each item as it is distributed. If the check register has additional columns available, a column may be assigned to an individual account for those accounts used most frequently. The miscellaneous column is used for items that do not occur frequently enough to warrant a column of their own. The items in each column should be summarized at the bottom, except for those columns assigned to a single account.

Account numbers should be designated to each specific account, as it will greatly facilitate the distribution of expenses in the check register. To simplify identification, these account numbers are usually assigned in different "hundred" or "thousand" groups to correspond to the different types of accounts:

General Fund

Physical Plant

401	Heat
402	Utilities
403	Salaries

General Fund

4010—1000	Heat—Church
4010—2000	Heat—School
4020—1000	Utilities—Church
4020—2000	Utilities—School

(See the sample chart of accounts in Exhibit 3-4 for more details.)

Whether it be a simple bookkeeping system or one using computers with a large volume of checks, a voucher-type check is highly recommended. This type of check has a voucher attached to it upon which the purpose of the payment is explained. A duplicate of each check can then be retained in the church's accounting files.

It is important that each column in the check register be completely filled in. If the check register you are using has the lines preprinted with check numbers, these numbers should not be ignored. The actual check number of each item should also be entered. At the end of the month, the columns in the check register should be totaled and a new page started for recording checks written in the following month. Any space remaining on the page can be used for recapping and other special comments.

Chart of Accounts

Every church bookkeeping system, no matter what the size, needs to have a proper chart of accounts. A chart of accounts is a formal listing of all the different accounts used by the church. Usually, the chart of accounts has numbers assigned to each account to help identify accounts and to more readily locate the account in the general ledger. Every account in the general ledger is listed in the chart of accounts—all assets, liabilities, income, and expenses. The chart of accounts is an index to facilitate bookkeeping.

It is impossible to provide a suggested chart of accounts that would be fully applicable in every situation. A small church does not need as elaborate a breakdown as is needed in a large church, and a church operating on a unified budget will have a chart of accounts that differs considerably from a church using a number of separate funds.

It does not matter whether the chart of accounts is large or small, the use of the account numbers is still important. Using an account number to identify an account will save a considerable amount of time and provide records that are neater and easier to follow.

The suggested chart of accounts provided in Exhibit 3-4 is for illustration purposes only and is based on a church with the following four funds:

> General Fund
>
> Missions Fund
>
> Building Fund
>
> Special Funds

The last of these, Special Funds, is really not one fund, but many funds created for special purposes and closed out when that purpose is accomplished. For example, taking a special offering for camp scholarships would create a special fund that will be eliminated as soon as the funds are disbursed as designated by the purpose of this offering.

The needs of a local church must be considered in setting up a chart of accounts. The method of breaking down general fund disbursements may be done in a number of ways. Just try to use a method that provides the most information with the least amount of detail.

The numbering system presented here is not "chiseled in stone," nor is it the last word in charts of accounts. It is only a guide. However, it is best to use a numbering system that groups the accounts according to logical divisions. A numbering system that allows for four digits instead of two or three allows for future growth or the addition of subaccounts without having to continually be changing the basic numbering system. (See Exhibit 3-4.)

Double Entry System

To this point we have been discussing journals relating to "single entry systems." In a single entry system, the journal becomes the place of original entry as well as the summarization of accounts. When a financial report is prepared, the treasurer must go through the journals for the months involved and add up the totals to arrive at the figures to be inserted in the report. This procedure is adequate for smaller churches and is usually used where personnel are not available who have accounting or double entry bookkeeping experience.

Where experienced people are available, or in larger church situations, a double entry system is highly desirable. In a double entry system, in addition to the journals that have already been discussed, a general journal is set up that is used for the purpose of opening entries, adjusting entries, and closing entries. Anyone familiar with double entry bookkeeping is familiar with a general journal. Each month the summary totals are posted from the journals to a general ledger. A general ledger contains a page for each account in the chart of accounts. Each of these pages contains a debit, credit, and balance column. Each month the debits and credits from the general journal, cash receipts journal, and disbursements journal (check register) are posted to the general ledger. After completion of the posting, an adding machine tape is run on the balances to make sure the general ledger is in balance.

The advantage of maintaining a general ledger is that all the information is automatically summarized on a regular basis. This facilitates the preparation of periodic financial reports and eliminates errors that may otherwise be made in accumulating figures. Although it is not essential to have a double entry system in order to maintain good accounting records for a church, it is highly desirable to do so whenever the opportunity is available.

The simplest form of double entry system includes the cash account as the only asset account. Other accounts are income or receipts and disbursements as have already been designated in the chart of accounts. Under this simplified form, liability accounts for mortgages are not established. Liability accounts would be established, however, for payroll taxes and other temporary liabilities that are automatically liquidated in the following month. Operating expenses are usually not accrued but are recorded as paid on a "cash" basis.

It is also possible to establish a general ledger that would include asset accounts for buildings, land, equipment, and any other asset held by the church. Liability accounts would be established for mortgages and other obligations.

Just a word of sympathy for those who have just read this section on double entry systems and are saying, "This is too complicated for me!" I was told years ago that a wise man realizes when he is getting in "over his head" and knows where to go to get help. Please don't reject a double entry system because you don't understand it. Get some professional assistance, and you'll see how helpful this system can be.

The choice of the proper system for a particular church depends on the size of the church, the availability of qualified personnel, the desires of the church organization regarding financial reporting, and other local factors.

Other Considerations

Financial Reports

Financial reporting is vitally important because information about the financial health of a ministry is often based on the information contained in such reports. Unfortunately, this area has not received a great deal of attention in the past and, in fact, has been frequently neglected. Because the church financial statements are considered key documents, certain common characteristics should be present in these statements. Robert Gray in his instructive book, *Managing the Church* (volume 2), makes the following recommendations:[8]

- They should be easily understood so that any member of the church who takes the time to study them will understand what they are saying. (This is the one characteristic that is the most frequently absent).

- They should be concise so that the person studying them will not get lost in detail.

- They should be all-inclusive and should embrace all activities of the church, such as church schools, summer camp, and so on. If there are two or three funds, the statement should clearly show the relationship between the funds without a lot of confusing detail.

- They should have a focal point for comparison. In most instances, this will be a comparison with the budget or figures from the corresponding period last year.

- They should be prepared on a timely basis. The longer the delay after the end of the period, the longer the period before corrective action can be taken.

Actually, these features could be applied to almost any type of business enterprise. (Unfortunately, most financial statements presented in churches follow the lines of inertia or tradition—"we've always done it that way!" A frequent problem is that the individual involved simply doesn't know what to do or how to do it.

One of the most frequent problems is that the volunteer engaged in financial responsibilities (doing the job on a part-time basis), does not have the time or the training to develop new or improved ways of presenting things, even if it would greatly benefit the church. Also, there is mixed reluctance on the part of the nonaccountant to make changes in financial statement formats because he lacks confidence in his ability to tinker with the "mysteries" of accounting. Furthermore, "just about the time the treasurer is really becoming familiar with church statements and could start to make meaningful changes, his term expires and he is replaced with someone else who has to start from scratch."[9]

One answer, then, is to develop a basic format and stay with it. Some financial reports are shown in Exhibits 3-5, 3-6, and 3-7. These examples aren't necessarily the final word in reports. Therefore, choose a format that suits your needs, or modify one of those provided in the exhibits. The actual statements to be used would vary depending on the type of information desired and the size of the ministry involved. One of the greatest contributions the treasurer can make is the development of an effective form of financial reporting so that the reports are understandable and meaningful to the reader.

---

8. Robert N. Gray, *Managing the Church* (New York: NCC Publication Services, 1977), 2:124.
9. Ibid., pp. 124-25.

Professional Advice

Many churches cannot afford outside accounting professionals. However, good resource people are usually available either within the congregation or certainly within the community. If you cannot afford to hire outside individuals to help you on a regular basis, at least use them as a reference when questions arise.

Annual Audit

The financial records of every church should be audited periodically. This is true whether the church is small or large. The basis for the audit is not a suspicion of incompetence or wrongdoing, nor should it be looked upon as an indication of distrust or a lack of confidence in those people handling funds. On the contrary, an audit is an honest, objective, and impersonal evaluation of the church's financial systems and procedures and its financial statements.

A complete audit should result in the detection of errors, deficiencies in certain policies, and gaps in procedures, whether intentional or through carelessness. It should also result in some type of formal recommendations to the church leadership as to areas where improvement in the church's procedures can be made. There are at least five advantages of an audit:

1. It helps to improve the church's financial reporting systems, procedures, and internal control.
2. It can result in suggestions for improvement of systems and procedures.
3. It can help a church avoid potential financial and legal problems.
4. It can result in improved church operations.
5. It provides assurance to the congregation and outsiders that the church's financial records are being properly maintained.

In those churches where the cost of an audit is prohibitive, the books should at least be examined by an audit committee appointed by the church from its membership. In many cases, the audit committee may consist of the finance committee, except for the elimination of the treasurer and financial secretary. The treasurer and financial secretary should be present when the audit is performed in order to locate items and to explain areas that are in question. They should not, however, be a part of the audit committee or have any responsibility directly related to it.

Normally, the audit should be conducted as soon as possible after the close of the fiscal year. After a time has been arranged, the financial secretary and treasurer should bring the records and supporting data to the committee for the audit.

The key phrase once again is internal control. When talking to an auditor or the audit committee, you should especially direct their attention to areas that are unusual or complex and where their expertise is needed or can be beneficial.

In selecting an auditor, try to look for a person or firm that either specializes in, or has experience in dealing with, nonprofit organizations.

Establishing a Fiscal Year

The setting of a fiscal year doesn't always have to coincide with the calendar year. The fiscal year should correspond with the organization's natural operating cycle. Aside from the common practice of adhering to the calendar year, there are at least two other possible alternatives:

1. A fiscal year that begins October 1 and ends September 30 can flow concurrently with the fall programming of the church. Furthermore, if your church conducts an annual pledge campaign, the best time to embark upon this drive would be in the fall, not during January when Christmas bills are being dealt with.

2. July 1 is another option, particularly for a large church. If an audit is conducted each year, July is a good time to start the process, while activity is low. It also frees staff people to close the books, prepare for the audit, and be ready for the increased church activities that pick up in the fall. Frequently, some accounting firms offer favorable rates for work performed during the summer months.

Conclusion

Well, there it is! I trust you have been either stimulated to make some improvements in your financial procedures or convinced even more that your fiscal house is in order. Whatever your situation, if you prove to be faithful in the handling of money, God will entrust you with even greater things.

"If . . . you have not been faithful in the use of unrighteous mammon, who will entrust the true riches to you" (Luke 16:11)?

SUMMARY OF RECEIPTS

DATE _____

OFFERING _____

ENVELOPES:

    GENERAL FUND $ _____

    MISSION FUND   _____

    BUILDING FUND   _____

    _____   _____

    _____   _____

TOTAL ENVELOPES   _____

    LOOSE   _____

GRAND TOTAL DEPOSITED   _____

COUNTED BY: _____

_____

_____

Exhibit 3-1

746   June 10, 1990   746

United Community Church
ATLANTA, GEORGIA
MY WEEKLY OFFERING
FOR THE ONGOING MINISTRY
OF MY CHURCH

Name _____ Amount $_____

AUG 4 1990

982   982

Growing
G
B
C
Mark '2 30-31
Together

Grace
Bible
Church

Anytown, USA 90021

$ _____

Name _____

Address _____

---

311   311

Thanksgiving

Amount $ _____

Name _____

Exhibit 3-2

DATE 1968	DESCRIPTION	DR CASH DEPOSITED	CR GENERAL FUND	CR MISSION FUND	CR BUILDING FUND	MISCELLANEOUS FUNDS - CR - PURPOSE	AMOUNT
Jan 7	Envelope Offering	685.42	385.90	200.36	102.16		
Jan 7	Loose Offering	6.814	6.814				
Jan 14	Envelope Offering	480.61	211.24	185.14	84.23		
Jan 14	Loose Offering	38.76	38.76				
Jan 17	Special Mid-Week Offering	72.71				Church Extension Offer.	72.71
Jan 21	Envelope Offering	732.14	368.33	232.67	131.14		
Jan 21	Loose Offering	82.19	82.19				
Jan 28	Envelope Offering	655.32	415.86	118.14	121.32		
Jan 28	Loose Offering	56.40	56.40				
	January Total	2876.69	1601.82	736.31	445.85		72.71

$2,876.69

AGREES

Exhibit 3-3

SUGGESTED CHART OF ACCOUNTS

FIRST CHRISTIAN CHURCH

Receipts

General Fund
301 Envelope Offerings
302 Loose Offerings
308 Interest on Savings Accounts
309 Miscellaneous Income

Mission Fund
321 Envelope Offerings
322 Special Offerings
329 Miscellaneous Income

Building Fund
341 Envelope Offerings
342 Special Offerings
349 Miscellaneous Income

Special Funds
361 Offerings
362 Special Gifts
363 Memorial Gifts
369 Miscellaneous Income

Disbursements

General Fund

Physical Plant
401 Heat
402 Utilities
403 Custodian Salaries
404 Social Security Tax
405 Janitorial Supplies
406 Insurance
407 Repair and Maintenance - Building and Grounds
408 Repair and Maintenance - Equipment

Exhibit 3-4

409 Telephone
410 Equipment
411 Bus Expense
412 Miscellaneous

Pastoral Ministry

421 Salary
422 Literature and Printing
423 Office Supplies
424 Pulpit Supply
425 Special Meetings Expense
426 Parsonage - Insurance
427 Pension Plan
428 Special Travel Allowances
429 Auto Allowance
430 Parsonage Utilities

Christian Education

441 Salary
442 Literature and Printing
443 Office Supplies
444 Pension Plan
445 Special Travel Allowances
446 Auto Allowance
447 Utilities Allowance

Worship Service

461 Music and Choir Expense
462 Literature and Printing
463 Office Supplies
464 Flowers

Miscellaneous General Expense

481 Special Gifts
482 Advertising
483 Office Salaries

Exhibit 3-4
continued

484   Social Security Tax
485   Flowers
486   Miscellaneous

Mission Fund
501   North American Baptist General Conference
502
(an account would be established and assigned an account number
 for each organization or person for which mission support is
 budgeted)

Building Fund
601   Construction Projects
602
(an account would be established and assigned an account number
 for each project)
621   Interest Expense
622   Principal Payments

Special Funds
701   Library Fund, etc.
(a separate account would be established for each fund which will
 not liquidate itself immediately)
721   Special Offerings
722   Special Gifts
723   Memorial Gifts

Exhibit 3-4
continued

FIRST CHURCH
Any Town, Any State

CASH RECONCILIATION
Year Ended December 31, 1969

	General Fund	Mission Fund	Building Fund	Special Funds	Total
Cash Balance - January 1, 1969					
National Bank - checking account	$ 1,242.16	$ - 0 -	$ 232.10	$ 864.32	$ 2,338
Savings account	- 0 -	- 0 -	5,000.00	- 0 -	5,000
Total Cash on Hand January 1, 1969	$ 1,242.16	$ - 0 -	$ 5,232.10	$ 864.32	$ 7,338
Cash Received During the Year	$24,114.10	$16,400.43	$10,382.16	$ 1,003.86	$51,900
Total Cash to Account For	$25,356.26	$16,400.43	$15,614.26	$ 1,868.18	$59,239
Cash Disbursed During the Year	24,073.14	16,400.43	9,882.41	1,222.26	51,578
Cash Balance - December 31, 1969	$ 1,283.12	$ - 0 -	$ 5,731.85	$ 645.92	$ 7,660
Made Up as Follows:					
National Bank - checking account	$ 1,283.12	$ - 0 -	$ 731.85	$ 645.92	$ 2,660
Savings account	- 0 -	- 0 -	5,000.00	- 0 -	5,000
Total Cash on Hand December 31, 1969	$ 1,283.12	$ - 0 -	$ 5,731.85	$ 645.92	$ 7,660

Exhibit 3-5

FIRST CHURCH
Any Town, Any State

GENERAL FUND DISBURSEMENTS
Year Ended December 31, 1969

Disbursements - General Fund	Budget	Actual	Over (Short)
Physical Plant:			
Utilities	$ 2,100.00	$ 2,069.14	$ (30.86)
Custodian salaries	3,200.00	3,200.00	- 0 -
Janitor supplies	270.00	232.14	(37.86)
Insurance	830.00	826.40	(3.60)
Repairs and maintenance	200.00	360.40	160.40
Equipment purchased	300.00	46.00	(254.00)
Bus expense	260.00	323.95	63.95
Miscellaneous	140.00	111.12	(28.88)
Total Physical Plant	$ 7,300.00	$ 7,169.15	$ (130.85)
Pastoral Ministry:			
Salary, housing allowance	$ 8,600.00	$ 8,600.00	- 0 -
Literature and printing	100.00	156.43	56.43
Office supplies	100.00	96.32	(3.68)
Pulpit supply	100.00	160.00	60.00
Pension plan - (10-12% approximately)	900.00	900.00	- 0 -
Auto allowance	900.00	900.00	- 0 -
Special travel allowances	150.00	317.32	167.32
Total Pastoral Ministry	$10,850.00	$11,130.07	$ 280.07
Christian Education:			
Salary	$ 1,800.00	$ 1,800.00	$ - 0 -
Literature and printing	50.00	13.08	(36.92)
Office supplies	50.00	16.09	(33.91)
Auto allowance	600.00	600.00	- 0 -
Total Christian Education	$ 2,500.00	$ 2,429.17	$ (70.83)
Worship and Service:			
Music and choir expense	$ 460.00	$ 432.16	$ (27.84)
Literature and printing	590.00	369.27	(220.73)
Office supplies	90.00	118.49	28.49
Flowers	60.00	62.42	2.42
Total Worship and Service	$ 1,200.00	$ 982.34	$ (217.66)

Exhibit 3-6

FIRST CHURCH
Any Town, Any State

GENERAL FUND RECEIPTS
Year Ended December 31, 1969

Receipts - General Fund	Budget	Actual	Over (Short)
Envelope offerings	$23,000.00	$22,294.89	$ (705.11)
Loose offerings	1,400.00	1,764.21	364.21
Miscellaneous income	60.00	55.00	(5.00)
Total Receipts	$24,460.00	$24,114.10	$ (345.90)
Percent Short of Budget			1.5%

Exhibit 3-7

Fundamentals of Budgeting

He who is slack in his work
Is brother to him who destroys.

(Proverbs 18:9)

"Who needs a budget?" someone might ask. "Let's just spend money as the Lord provides. If God is in it, He will supply!" One prominent pastor said, "Budgets limit God." But do they? Does a budget really stifle the work of the Holy Spirit in the local church?

The reality of the issue is that, for a church to be successful in managing its financial resources, budgets are an absolute necessity. Although most people in church leadership recognize this fact, many consider budgets a necessary evil. That's usually because the perception or philosophy behind budgeting isn't clearly understood. Often budgets are viewed as merely a method of exercising financial restraint and control—they have a negative connotation.

Budgets when viewed properly are control mechanisms. But, more than that, they are a planning tool and an operational guide to help the local church achieve its short- and long-range objectives. Webster defines a *budget* as "an estimate of future financial income and outgo." As cold and as sterile as that may sound, church financial officers should view it as an opportunity to look ahead—to make plans.

The budget doesn't dictate what is to be done; it is supposed to conform to *your* plans. You are in control! Luke 14:28 tells us that before a man builds a tower, he sits down and counts the cost. You need to decide if you actually need to build a "tower" in the first place. Simply because you can afford to build, add staff, enlarge the worship center, start a day school, or whatever the endeavor, counting the cost should include maintenance of the "tower" or support expenses for these new projects.

The point is, decide ahead of time what you want to do. Once you feel sure of your need, ask yourself, "Can we afford this now? What about six months from now, when we have to hire an additional tower janitor? What about heating and lighting the tower?" This additional planning isn't supposed to discourage you in what you believe God would have you to do. But counting the cost means counting *all* the conceivable costs—both current and future.

Simply stated, plan carefully first, budget second.

The Overview Process

An effective budgeting process requires two important elements.

Looking Back

Past giving patterns are important in helping you determine whether you can afford to fund what you believe is needed. This information can often demonstrate past trends relating to spending, expenses, and costs connected with ministry thrusts (i.e., building programs, missions emphasis). For instance, in the area of giving, how much have offerings increased over the last three years? Can you expect this trend to continue? Why? You will have to do your homework in this area to arrive at usable figures. However, by using records from the past (canceled checks, bankbooks, ledgers, or other financial records), you can develop a simple profile of past performance. (See Exhibit 4-1.)

Looking Ahead

Budgets or projections are plans expressed in numbers—they are future needs set to figures. Since budgets are customarily designed to accommodate a twelve-month period, long-range plans must be accounted for in the process, lest, as our passage in Luke points out, "when he has laid a foundation, and is not able to finish, all who observe it begin to ridicule him."

Goals for your church are essential to good budgeting. A pastor was overheard to have said, "We prepare a budget every year but practically abandon it after six months because things tend to change so much." That is a result of poor planning or making a budget so tight and restrictive that unforeseen events are not accounted for. Therefore, in your planning process, allow for the unexpected by setting aside funds into contingency accounts. That too is a part of planning ahead!

The formation of a planning group to establish goals for the next one to three years is extremely important. Budgeting should not consist of simply adding 10 percent across-the-board to last year's budget. Ask yourself, "Where are we now, and where do we want to go?"

Additionally, determine, to the best of your ability, what the local economy will be like in the next twelve months. There are several sources you can turn to for this information. Many large banks produce an annual, local economic outlook report. State and city governments also have their own "educated guesses" of future economic conditions available. They too need to plan their budgets based on expected "contributions"—taxes.

Finally, the question of whether your congregation can handle an increase in their financial commitment needs to be addressed. Perhaps a 10 percent increase in the church budget would realistically exceed the ability of the people to meet that requirement.

There are those who would argue that people need to be "stretched," to "step out on faith," to be challenged. However, church leaders need to keep in mind that there is a fine line between faith and presumption. Many churches "write checks" and then ask God to "cash" them. Often a church that wants to undertake a project will go ahead and put it in the budget—a "faith budget"—even though it may require a 15 percent increase in giving over the next year, when in fact, the giving has been increasing only 6 percent for the last three years.

The scenario here is all too common. The result is that the pastor will have the task of convincing the people that they need to increase their giving to meet the new budget. This results in more "pulpit time" being devoted to the subject of money and budgets, especially if giving falls short of the projections. Also, if the budgeted items are purchased, a cash flow shortage develops, which in turn puts more pressure on the congregation. The next logical step is to cut back ongoing ministries in order to pay the bills already incurred for the new project.

Without a question, there certainly is a place for faith when it comes to giving. However, the faith challenge needs to be realistic and within the capability of a local congregation to meet the need. That is why looking back at past performance and then looking ahead with an understanding of the basic economic factors that affect giving will go a long way toward producing a budget that will allow people to both *stretch* and *reach* the goal.

The Production Process

Many aspiring young preachers have been given the K.I.S.S. principle—the polite spelled-out version of which is "Keep It Simple, Saint!" That's good advice for those preparing an annual budget as well. Make the budget simple and easy to understand. Even if the church is large, the projections can still be kept in elementary terms and understandable to the average church member. It doesn't matter how big your church is, the basic format can still be the same.

First Step—Departments

Reduce the entire church structure into departments (i.e., Music, Youth, Facilities). Each area of ministry is to be assigned either a staff person, if the church is large, or a lay person. This individual is responsible for projecting the income, if there is any, and the expense portion of the budget.

Second Step—Line-Items

Each department should have "line-items" assigned to the revenue and expense portion of the budget. This means that every conceivable type of expense should have a category and be placed within the budget. For example, Youth Ministry could have a separate line entry labeled "Publications and Materials" for items such as quarterlies, Sunday school papers, maps, and songbooks. When several items are similar, they can be grouped together under a single line-item. Using our Youth Ministry as an example, you might place Publications and Materials in with Equipment (such as slide projectors and visual aids) and title them both as "Teaching Aids" or "Material and Equipment." If the church is quite small, simply put all youth-related expenses under one heading—Youth.

The line-item method allows you the freedom to be as detailed as you choose. You can plan for and track any segment of the church budget you desire. A word of caution though—don't get too general and lump everything together into as few categories as possible. That only defeats the purpose of planning and control.

The point is, every expected expense should be placed into a department line-item. This will prevent funds or expenses from "falling through the cracks."

Third Step—Revenue and Expense

If you expect to charge for an item or event, list it as both a revenue *and* expense item. It is important to plan for money coming in as well as for those funds being spent.

Fourth Step—Chart of Accounts

Assign numbers to your departments and line-items. The listing of these numbers is commonly called a Chart of Accounts. (See section 3.)

Format—Large Church

The format for a large church may look like Exhibit 4-2.

Format—Smaller Church

A smaller church may want to a follow a simpler, more general format. Exhibit 4-3 shows a basic, simple budget that can be expanded by adding more line-items. The sample can also be reduced by grouping all similar line-items into one line-item. For example, a smaller church would have one line-item for salaries and expenses instead of breaking this category out by department as is the case in a larger church. This example is only an aid, and you should not hesitate to make changes where they are appropriate.

Worksheets

Worksheets can also be helpful in the preliminary steps of gathering data and then summarizing the budget information. Sample worksheets are presented in Exhibits 4-4, 4-5, 4-6, and 4-7. Department heads, as well as members of the Finance Committee, will find these useful.

Although the first time you prepare a budget using these methods may require a lot of effort, the next time will be much simpler. Even though using this new procedure could result in many more line-item entries than you had in past budgets, it will still be easier to track income and expenses with the department/line-item method.

The Presentation Process

There is one thing you want to avoid in presenting budgets to the church leadership or to the congregation—surprises! An open and honest approach will avoid suspicion and a confrontational atmosphere. How do you accomplish this? By adopting a "flow of cooperation" within the entire organization. The process is as follows.

The Assembly Line

The department heads assemble their own projections based on past experience, plus what they feel will be needed to carry on the ministry in their specific area. The purpose is to include the people who have the responsibility of overseeing their particular ministry in the budgeting process.

With an autocratic or nonparticipative organization, be it a church or a business, top management sets the budgets, issues them to "operations managers," and then holds the managers accountable for meeting them. The organization managers (department heads) must then work within the budgetary guidelines to meet their stated goals. On the other hand, with participative budgeting, department heads submit individual budgets. Top management analyzes the projections using some of the techniques mentioned earlier. They also discuss and modify those budgets (when necessary, with the participation of department heads) and combine them into the overall budget.

Therefore, for budgeting to be effectively used as a *coordinating* tool, it must be a participative system. When all the people who are responsible for managing the finances of their ministry are allowed to participate in the budget preparation process, the entire organization can benefit. Estimates of what the church can achieve the next year, and at what cost, are usually more realistic with a participative system than if those at the top make the projections alone.

However, it must be remembered that department heads participating in the budgeting process will no doubt place their own personal desires for their ministry as a priority. These personal goals cannot be allowed to be the primary motivation for their projections. A church must make sure that the goals of the department heads and those of the church can be reached simultaneously. If this relationship is not clear, department heads might be tempted to inflate their projections at the expense of the overall church objectives.

Advantages of a participative budget include:

- Improved initiative, morale, and enthusiasm
- A more realistic budget plan
- Properly delegated responsibility that is more readily accepted
- Increased interdepartmental cooperation
- A higher degree of awareness at all levels
- A sense of "ownership" of the entire budget and not just a special interest area

The most effective budgets are those that originate at the bottom of the organizational ladder. This bottom-up approach is the key element that leads to accuracy, relevance, and the ultimate success of the budget. The actual procedures used in budget development and the end uses of the budget are equally important.

Inspectors

After a first draft proposal has been submitted from the departments, the budget goes to a Finance Committee. This group of individuals, who are *not* department heads, reviews the soundness of the submitted budgets as a whole. It is this committee's job to determine if the church can, in fact, meet the projections. This evaluation, as mentioned before, is based on the local economy, past giving patterns, and an assessment of the members' ability to support the new budget.

If the projections are beyond what the Finance Committee believes to be attainable, then the budgets are returned to the department heads with suggestions for reductions, and they may take appropriate action. Again, the goal is cooperation through participation. If specific cuts can be made, then they need to be made by the departments and not the Finance Committee. If all the departments cannot reduce their budgets to a satisfactory level, then the pastor needs to be informed. He may decide to go to the congregation, after the budget is approved in its present form, and challenge them to a greater financial commitment. However, if the senior pastor doesn't wish to do this, then the Finance Committee may have to make the needed reductions to balance the budget. Any cuts that are made at this point must be clearly within the guidelines of the stated priorities of the church. They may be in specific departments or across-the-board cuts, the decision being the Finance Committee's.

The Rollout

Once approved by the Finance Committee, the budget goes to the church's ruling board for acceptance. If a congregational vote is required, now is the time to call a special budget meeting, with every interested church member invited to attend. The purpose of this meeting is for information only, sort of an open forum. It is not intended to be a time for final adoption of the budget. Hopefully, once all the questions and issues have been satisfactorily dealt with, the general congregational meeting can convene the next week. At this meeting, the budget can then be approved by the people. This is merely an opportunity for questions and answers. If there is someone who has a question about a specific item and a point of clarification would be long and involved, speak with this person during the following week—if possible on a one-to-one basis. Make every effort, though, to move the process along, avoiding debates and confrontations. (See Exhibit 4-8.)

Conclusion

Although blank sample budget forms listing general categories and line-items are presented in Exhibit 4-5, it is the general format that is always important. Church leaders and congregations generally want to know the following information:

1. What was our giving last year?
2. What was last year's budget?
3. Did we accomplish the projections or miss them? By how much?
4. What is the projected giving for the new budget year?
5. What is the new budget?
6. What are the major categories?
7. Do the leaders expect us to achieve our goal?

The budget can illustrate all these points in whatever form you choose. You can use a formal line-item budget, pie charts, graphs, or even a narrative summary. There is no hard, fast rule when it comes to illustrating a budget. Again, I would suggest that it be kept simple.

One last principle: Don't allow budgets to be the absolute final word. Conditions can change, and it may be necessary to increase or decrease projections. Maybe it would be best to move some of the line-items around to adapt to present conditions. The point is, don't allow the ministry of the church to become a slave to the numbers in the budget. The tail shouldn't wag the dog! As stated earlier, the budget is simply a road map, but don't take too many detours.

"Do all things decently and in order," the Bible tells us (1 Corinthians 14:40, KJV*)—good advice, particularly when applied to the area of church budgets. To insure a smooth and orderly process, those entrusted with the responsibility of preparing the budget must do their homework. The presentation should be accurate, simple, and meaningful. The annual budget meeting should be a time of festiveness, not fighting, and caring instead of quarreling.

All in favor, say, "Aye!"

*King James Version.

FIRST CHRISTIAN CHURCH

Income – 1985 to 1990

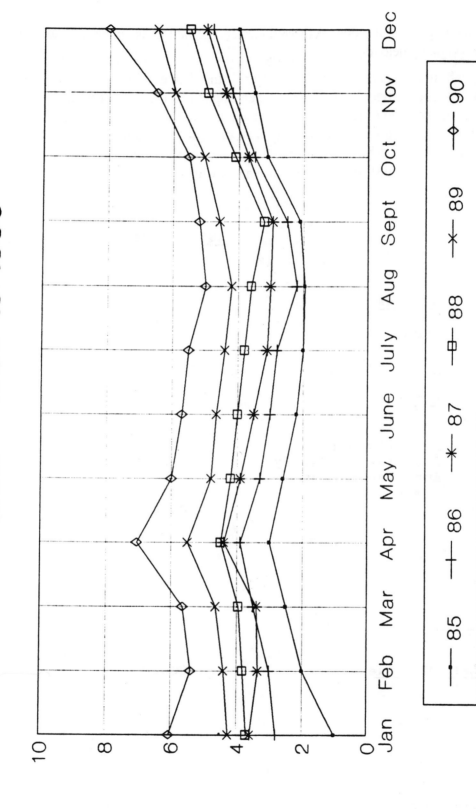

Fiscal Year Ending December 31

Exhibit 4-1

The format for a large church may look like this:

YOUTH DEPARTMENT - #202

Annual Budget

		1986 Actual	1987 Projected
	Revenue		
3322	Camps	----------	----------
	Total Revenue	----------	----------
	Expenses		
6202	Pastor's Salary	000000	000000
6203	Secretary's Salary	000000	000000
6204	Employee Expenses	000000	000000
6205	Camps	000000	000000
6206	Curriculum	000000	000000
6207			
6208			
6209			
6210			
Total Expenses		000000	000000
Total Less Revenue		000000	000000

Exhibit 4-2

A smaller church may want to a follow a simpler, more general format:

CHRISTIAN EDUCATION - #200

Annual Budget

		1986 Actual	1987 Projected
	Revenue		
3322	Camps	----------	----------
3352	Banquets	----------	----------
	Total Revenue	----------	----------
	Expenses		
4412	Salaries & Expenses	000000	000000
4422	Literature & Printing	000000	000000
2282	Camps	000000	000000
4572	Banquets	000000	000000
4485			
4490			
4495			
Total Expenses		000000	000000
Total Less Revenue		000000	000000

Exhibit 4-3

FIRST CHURCH - ANNUAL BUDGET - 1987

RECEIPTS	1986	Proposed 1987	Difference (+ or -)

General Offerings

4100	General Offerings	95000	105000	10000
4150	Interest of Savings Acct	500	500	0
4200	Miscellaneous Income	300	300	0
	Total General Offerings	95800	105800	10000

Designated Receipts

3100	Missions	12000	13200	1200
3150	Organ Fund	500	500	0
3250	Debt Retirement	12000	12000	0
3300	Camps	1000	1100	100
3350	Banquets	1000	1000	0
3400	Other	75	75	0
	Total Designated Offerings	26575	27875	1300

TOTAL RECEIPTS	122375	133675	11300

DISBURSEMENTS

Physical Plant

4010	Heat	4000	4500	500
4020	Utilities	2500	3300	800
4030	Custodial Services	4400	4600	200
4040	Social Security Taxes	485	514	29
4050	Janitorial Supplies	300	325	25
4060	Insurance	1200	1250	50
4070	Repair & Maintenance	2000	2000	0
4080	Repair & Maint -Equip	1000	1000	0
4090	Telephone	3000	3500	500
4100	Equipment	500	500	0
4110	Bus Expense	1500	1700	200
4120	Miscellaneous	100	100	0
	Total Physical Plant	20985	23289	2304

Exhibit 4-4

Christian Education

4410	Salary (All Pastors)	45000	47700	2700
4420	Literature & Print	600	650	50
4430	Office Supplies	200	215	15
4440	Pension Plan	1200	1250	50
4450	Special Travel Allowance	500	500	0
4470	Camps	1200	1400	200
	Total Christian Education	48700	51715	3015

Worship Service

4610	Music & Choir Expense	900	950	50
4620	Literature & Printing	1200	1250	50
4630	Office Supplies	500	500	0
4640	Flowers	1500	1600	0
	Total Worship Service	4100	4300	100

Misc. General Expense

4810	Special Gifts	300	300	0
4820	Advertising	300	325	25
4830	Office Salaries	20000	22000	2000
4840	Social Security Tax	1440	1515	75
4850	Banquets	300	300	0
4860	Miscellaneous	500	500	0
	Total Misc Gen Expense	22840	24940	2100

Missions Expense

5010	No. American Mission Conf	8000	9000	1000
5020	Any org. or individual	3000	3500	500
	Total Mission Expense	11000	12500	1500

Building Fund

6010	Construction Projects	3000	3000	0
6020	(each project would be given a line-item)			0
6210	Interest Expense	1200	1200	0
6220	Principle Payments	12000	12000	0
	Total Building Fund	16200	16200	0

TOTAL DISBURSEMENTS	123825	132944	9019

SURPLUS OR DEFICIT	-1450	731	2281

Exhibit 4-4
continued

Sample Budget Form

		Current	Proposed
I.	World Missions Ministries		
	Cooperative Program	_____	_____
	Associational Missions	_____	_____
	Direct Missions	_____	_____
	Children's Home	_____	_____
	Local Missions	_____	_____
	Total	_____	_____
II.	Pastoral Ministries		
	Pastor's Salary	_____	_____
	Housing & Utilities	_____	_____
	Associate Pastor's Salary	_____	_____
	Housing & Utilities	_____	_____
	Secretary	_____	_____
	Radio & Television	_____	_____
	Deacon Care Program	_____	_____
	Revival	_____	_____
	Total	_____	_____
III.	Education Ministries		
	Minister of Education's Salary	_____	_____
	Housing & Utilities	_____	_____
	Secretary	_____	_____
	Sunday School	_____	_____
	Church Training	_____	_____
	Brotherhood	_____	_____
	Woman's Missionary Union	_____	_____
	Leadership Training	_____	_____
	Total	_____	_____
IV.	Music and Worship Ministries		
	Minister of Music's Salary	_____	_____
	Housing & Utilities	_____	_____
	Organist's Salary	_____	_____
	Music & Supplies	_____	_____
	Special Programs	_____	_____
	Worship Supplies	_____	_____
	Total	_____	_____

Budget Worksheets from *Church Administration Handbook*, edited by Bruce Powers. Chapter entitled *Financial Procedures* by Mark Short, Broadman Press, Nashville, Tennessee. Copyright 1985.

Exhibit 4-5

V. Support Ministries

V. Support Ministries
Library _____ _____
Recreation _____ _____
Church Secretary's Salary _____ _____
Office Supplies/Postage _____ _____
Stewardship/Budget Development _____ _____
Auditing/Financial Records _____ _____
Travel Expense (all staff) _____ _____
Convention expense (all staff) _____ _____
Annuity Payments _____ _____
Social Security _____ _____
Special Events _____ _____
Kitchen operation/supplies _____ _____
Total _____ _____

VI. Buildings and Grounds
Janitor's Salary _____ _____
Utilities _____ _____
Insurance _____ _____
Repairs _____ _____
Taxes _____ _____
Supplies _____ _____
Debt Retirement _____ _____
New Facilities _____ _____
Total _____ _____

Summary by Categories
I. World Missions Ministries _____ _____
II. Pastoral Ministries _____ _____
III. Education Ministries _____ _____
IV. Music and Worship Ministries _____ _____
V. Support Ministries _____ _____
VI. Buildings and Grounds _____ _____
Grand Total _____ _____

Exhibit 4-5
continued

Budget Work Sheet

	Current Budget-19XX	Actual/Anticipated Totals This Year	Committee Requests	Proposed Budget-19XX
Undesignated Receipts	$_____	$_____	$_____	$_____
DISBURSEMENTS				
Missions				
Cooperative Program	_____	_____	_____	_____
Associational Missions	_____	_____	_____	_____
Local	_____	_____	_____	_____
Total Missions	$_____	$_____	$_____	$_____
Educational Ministry				
Sunday School & Church Training	_____	_____	_____	_____
Vacation Bible School	_____	_____	_____	_____
Woman's Missionary Union	_____	_____	_____	_____
Brotherhood	_____	_____	_____	_____
Youth	_____	_____	_____	_____
Total Education	$_____	$_____	$_____	$_____
Property	$_____	$_____	$_____	$_____
Debt Retirement	$_____	$_____	$_____	$_____
General Operations				
Car Allowances	_____	_____	_____	_____
Conventions	_____	_____	_____	_____
Denominational Retirement	_____	_____	_____	_____
Insurance	_____	_____	_____	_____
Kitchen	_____	_____	_____	_____
Music & Equipment	_____	_____	_____	_____
Office Equipment	_____	_____	_____	_____
Postage	_____	_____	_____	_____
Church Supplies	_____	_____	_____	_____
Payroll Taxes	_____	_____	_____	_____
Utilities	_____	_____	_____	_____
Contingencies	_____	_____	_____	_____
Total General	$_____	$_____	$_____	$_____
Personnel				
Pastor	_____	_____	_____	_____
Church Secretary (part-time)	_____	_____	_____	_____
Janitor (part-time)	_____	_____	_____	_____
Total Personnel	$_____	$_____	$_____	$_____
Total Disbursements	$_____	$_____	$_____	$_____

Exhibit 4-6

Worksheet for Financial Support of the Minister

(Duplicate and use a separate sheet for each staff member.)

		This Year	Proposed for Next Year
I.	Ministry-Related Expenses		
	1. Automobile Allowance	_____	_____
	2. Convention Allowance	_____	_____
	3. Book Allowance	_____	_____
	4. Continuing Education Allowance	_____	_____
	5. Hospitality Allowance	_____	_____
	TOTAL EXPENSES	_____	_____
II.	Protection Benefits		
	1. Insurance		
	a. Life	_____	_____
	b. Long-Term Disability	_____	_____
	c. Medical	_____	_____
	2. Retirement	_____	_____
	TOTAL BENEFITS	_____	_____
III.	Basic Compensation Personal Support		
	1. Cash Salary	_____	_____
	2. Housing Allowance	_____	_____
	TOTAL COMPENSATION	_____	_____

Exhibit 4-7

THE PRODUCTION PROCESS

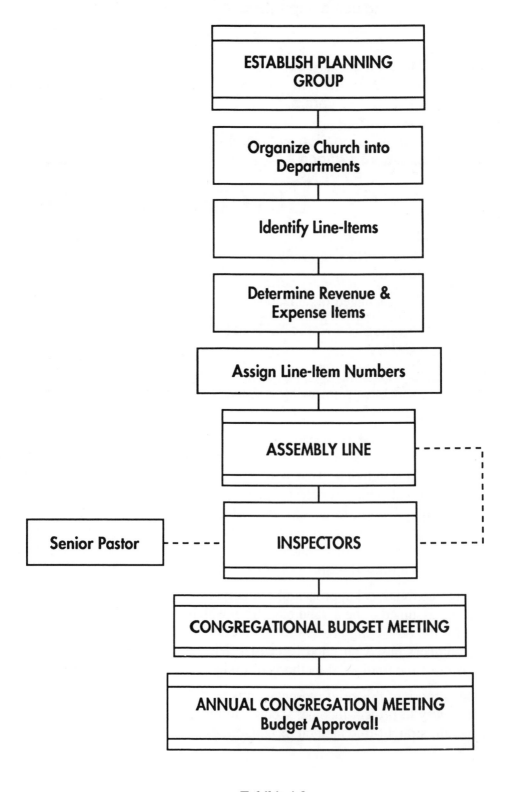

ESTABLISH PLANNING GROUP

Organize Church into Departments

Identify Line-Items

Determine Revenue & Expense Items

Assign Line-Item Numbers

ASSEMBLY LINE

Senior Pastor — — — INSPECTORS

CONGREGATIONAL BUDGET MEETING

ANNUAL CONGREGATION MEETING
Budget Approval!

Exhibit 4-8

Budgeting and Forecasting— Beyond the Basics

W*ebster's New World Dictionary* defines *status quo* as "the existing state of affairs." All well-managed organizations continually seek for ways to improve their status quo—that is, their existing financial state of affairs. This is accomplished by better regulating costs. Ministries experiencing slow growth implement cost control as a necessity for survival, while rapid growth ministries curb costs to ensure proper allocation of income to support continued success. For both types of ministries, budgeting provides the framework to reduce expenses while deriving the most benefits from available funds.

It's been said before, and it bears repeating, that budgeting ought to be an extension of strategic planning. Managers should scrutinize the business operations of their ministry from a cost-benefit standpoint. That will determine which activities should be reduced or eliminated and which should be given priority to receive more funds. Too often, however, ministries fail to go this extra step. They tend to do things the way they always have in the past, maintaining the status quo. This is not necessarily a criticism, because most churches use volunteer financial people to handle forecasting and budgeting, and it's on a limited basis.

Furthermore, the conventional approach to budgeting often fails. That is because previous budgets are assumed to be a valid base from which to start. But that isn't always true. In order for the budgeting process to be an effective tool, it is necessary to operate with real numbers based on good forecasts. What is needed is the ability to get beyond the basics of the traditional methods of budgeting.

Therefore, the purpose of this brief presentation is twofold: first, to demonstrate a simple but effective way to project income; second, to provide alternatives to the customary, twelve-month, straight-line method of budgeting.

Forecasting

Let's start with the concept of forecasting. It has been said that forecasting is more art than science. In other words, a good forecaster "guesses good!" As you prepare a forecast, you should look at as many approaches as possible, consider the trends, new developments, cycles, and anything else that might give you ideas.

One of the toughest forecasting jobs is that of the weather forecaster. Meteorologists observe wind patterns, satellite pictures, air pressure, and years of past trends. Each forecast is based on careful analysis of what is going on, why, and (more important) how it applies to the future. Their forecasts, like those of financial managers, are professional guesses based on knowledge, experience, and common sense. Obviously, we can't consult the Wharton School of Economics, the UCLA Econometric Model, or any other highly developed forecasting method. Even these methods are not 100 percent accurate. Aside from this, the church is a nonprofit corporation, and many of those reports are slanted toward the large corporations, which need high level, sophisticated data to assist them in making major financial decisions. This information is rooted in theories and studies involving macro- and microeconomics and is beyond the scope of most local churches.

However, there are some basic forecasting tools that we *can* put to use in our local churches. As a start, projecting income is certainly important. After all, what use is an expense budget if the income falls considerably short of the goal? This doesn't mean you lack faith or have "fallen from grace." I've known church leaders who felt they were out of God's will if they did not raise their budget each year. Of course, they always fell short—but that wasn't the point. At least their budget kept increasing! Meanwhile, the pastor had to continually keep asking people to give more money to "meet the budget." And then the people would complain because, "the pastor talks about money too much!" That is a common complaint about pastors.

At this point, we need to spend a few moments to examine the practice of forecasting a little more closely. The goal should be to develop a budget that uses real numbers and has meaning.

The Way It Was

Previous giving patterns are helpful in determining whether the present budget is feasible. Past spending shows expenses and costs connected with certain ministry thrusts. For example, what impact did a building or missions emphasis have on giving and expenses? Ask yourself questions. How much have offerings increased over the last three years? Can you expect this trend to continue? Why? You will have to do your homework in this area to arrive at usable figures. However, by using records from the past (canceled checks, bankbooks, ledgers, or other financial records), you can develop a simple profile of past performance.

Therefore, there are two features to look for when examining past income and expenses:

1. *Trends.* Exhibit 5-1 illustrates highs and lows in past giving patterns. Many giving peaks can be attributable to year-end tax donations, higher attendance at Easter, or other special holiday giving. The low points can be attributed to family Christmas holiday bills coming due near the first of the year or to post-year-end, tax-related giving or to the traditional summer slump.

   Expenses should then be accounted for based on past trends. It's simply a question of cash flow management during the peaks and valleys.

2. *The "X" Factor.* Previous financial activity may also reveal what could be called the "X" Factor. The "X" might be a major building-fund emphasis that affects cash available for general expenses, or it might be the death or resignation of the senior pastor, a fire, a church split, or any unforeseen problem or factor that significantly affects income.

Back to the Future

Often occurrences outside the realm of the church can seriously impact income and expenses—circumstances we have no control over that still affect the bottom line. Events in the general economy can determine the direction of many of your church's ministries.

For example, a higher inflation rate will affect variable home mortgage rates. For those families with these types of mortgages, less discretionary income will be available. A $100,000 thirty-year mortgage at 10.5 percent interest that increases to 11 percent results in a $450 annual increase. And that is only one half of one percent! The financial leadership of a suburban church needs to keep this in the back of their minds when they hear reports of the "prime rate" going up.

A dramatic increase in the price of oil might affect your church utility expenses. Attendance at services other than on Sunday mornings could drop as gasoline prices increase.

Therefore, some of the more significant aspects to look for in forecasting are economic conditions and new programs that can deflect giving from current needs.

- *Inflation.* People put more money into savings accounts because things cost more; interest rates on savings accounts go up, and uncertainty breeds economic conservativeness.
- *Weather.* Agriculture obviously is impacted when there is a drought, severe cold, or too much rain. Depending on the harvest conditions, giving could rise or drop.
- *Industrial Shifts.* Cities with economies tied to certain industries can be seriously affected by the health of those businesses. Knowing the economic outlook as it relates to the health of these companies would be a wise piece of information to have on hand at forecasting time.

• *A Building Program.* Generally speaking, a building program will create a deflection away from the General Fund. Gifts are often designated to the Building Fund despite the pastor's encouragement to make this type of giving over and above regular contributions. Experience has shown that this kind of giving—"deflective giving"—can pull anywhere from 18 to 25 percent of funds away from the general needs of the church. Again, a wise forecaster will take this into consideration.

The best forecast combines good, accurate information and management with common sense. Still, forecasting is an uncertain process. However, for a financial manager to ignore past trends or events in the general economy would be shortsighted and foolish.

Once you have the concept of forecasting and many of the details relating to your specific situation available, it is advisable to prepare a pro forma accounting statement. A pro forma statement is similar to what corporations refer to as a business plan. It's really a model of what the numbers for your church are supposed to look like over the next year (in some cases three years). The pro forma statement would be a cash flow plan—a model of your balance sheet as it would look if the cash flow and future revenues worked out the way you forecasted them.

Forecasting is a significant building block in budgeting for a church. It is an integral part of planning, budgeting, and finance.

Financial Budgets

Every ministry needs to make decisions about where it is going to place its financial resources. The disadvantage a nonprofit organization (a church in particular) has, is that it lacks the essential motive to earn a profit. Obviously, it isn't supposed to seek a profit—that isn't the point. In business, however, the profit is a standard, or measuring device, to determine the effectiveness of the company's efforts.

Churches, on the other hand, must have more indirect priorities or diffuse goals. Profit as an ongoing measure of their effectiveness is lost as a tool of management. (That is one of the reasons so many churches are wasteful when it comes to handling money.) Hence, the nonprofit organization must find another method to quantify success, control its operations, evaluate individual performances, and make resource allocation decisions.

A local church requires a specific planning process for setting goals, determining cash spending patterns, and deciding what program services will be provided. These plans should be formulated prior to the annual budget. Many churches traditionally look at how much money they estimate will be available and then look at existing programs to determine if they can afford to continue or increase them. Again, it's sort of a status quo method of budgeting.

An objective examination of the budgeting process within the traditional church context shows that there are some inherent weaknesses in the status quo method. Some of these deficiencies show themselves to be characteristics that work against an effective budgeting process:

- *Budget planning*. A church needs to determine priorities of ministry because there is no other way to measure the effective use of funds (i.e., earning a profit).
- *Revenue Budgeting*. Churches have special difficulties in the recognition and budgeting of revenues.
- *Expense Budgeting*. In preparing and using expense budgets, churches often find it difficult to match expenses incurred in delivery of services to those revenues that support those services.
- *Measuring Effectiveness and Control*. Most churches have difficulty measuring effectiveness in meeting budgeted service levels.
- *Budget Adaptability*. Church budgets are often difficult to modify once established. From year to year, budget allocations tend to be determined on an incremental basis.
- *Budget Participants*. The nonprofit budgeting process involves participants who have widely varying backgrounds and objectives.
- *Church Structure*. The church organizational structure often impedes the development of an effective budgeting system.[10]

Projecting cash flow relating to revenue and expenses is fundamental to the church's ability to plan and budget resources. You simply cannot effectively plan a church without planning its finances, which in essence is the purpose of forecasting.

Beyond the Basics

Before we move forward, we need to be sure a few assumptions are firmly in place.

1. The value and justification of a church budget is well accepted.
2. Budgets are a necessary management tool.
3. Furthermore, it should be understood that budgets are more than a control mechanism. They provide an invaluable device for measuring goals while monitoring for a minimum of overexpenditure and waste.

With this in mind, the next step beyond the basics of budgeting has to do with the refining process. The majority of churches in America use a flat-line, twelve-month budget model. (See Exhibit 5-2.) This is practical only if income and expenses are predictable from year to year. Churches experiencing a small amount of steady growth can accommodate a flat-line or fixed budget. However, churches with rapid growth, various start-up ministries, and volatile external "X" factors might consider a flexible budget or even the modified zero-based budget approach.

10. Adapted from H. W. Sweeny and Robert Rachlin, *Handbook of Budgeting* (New York: John Wiley, 1981).

The Fixed Budget

This is the most common church budget. In government or large nonprofit organizations it is sometimes referred to as an appropriation budget. Generally speaking, it is established for a definite period of time in advance and is not subject to change or alteration during the budget period (unless the leadership of the church decides to offer supplementary changes).

The fixed budget is useful when the church leaders are reasonably certain that conditions of income and expense will remain constant. No significant deviations from the forecast are expected. In this case, the additional time and expense of developing alternative or more refined budgets is unnecessary.

The fixed or traditional budget is based on a single best estimate of income and costs. A figure is determined that represents income for a total year. This amount, along with last year's expenditure total, is then divided by twelve. The result is an annual twelve-month budget in twelve equal periods.

The Flexible Budget

The flexible budget, in contrast, is especially suited for those churches in which operating costs are variable at different time periods or levels of activity. As a manager, you need to know that a flexible budget will require more of your time in the forecasting and monitoring phases.

Additionally, a flexible budget means managers need to be aware of line-item costs. The advantage, though, is that it permits all individual cost items to be "flexed" and altered to accommodate variations.

The advantages of flexible budgeting far outweigh the drawbacks:

- *Ability to Update*. Church leadership and department heads are not required to work with an outdated or unrealistic budget. Sudden economic shifts, resulting in many of the aspects mentioned in the section on forecasting, can occur. Under these circumstances, fixed budgets can become difficult to work with and in some cases are useless.

- *Provides for Opportunities*. Fixed budgets prevent the church from taking full advantage of opportunities that suddenly arise. New ministry opportunities are often met with resistance and the age-old reminder "It's not in the budget!" Flexible budgets permit leadership to adapt to and even capitalize on these open doors.

- *Realistic Guidelines*. With a flexible budget, the increase and decrease of income and expenses are the control mechanisms used for decision making, not the fixed budget that was established perhaps months ago. A flexible budget allows the church leadership the freedom to change directions as circumstances dictate.

For our purposes, we will examine two common varieties of the flexible budget concept.

1. Simple-Average Flexible Budget

In this type of budget model, the same three estimates of income and costs are developed and then averaged. For example, giving for the month of February based on past estimates could realistically be one of three figures: $100,000, $110,000, or $115,000. These three projections would then be charted with the average being $108,000. (See Exhibit 5-3.)

The main disadvantage to this method is that the financial manager is assigning an equal weight to each of the projections. It is three separate but equal scenarios. Although this is unlikely, the simple-average flexible budget is the simplest to prepare and present for approval. That is because the preparation time is shorter. Also, it is less complicated and therefore easier to understand and present for approval.

Although this type of budget shows a projection for revenue, it naturally follows that the same variations in income also follow for the expense side. If contributions are expected to rise and fall, then expenses should also be budgeted to coincide with the income stream. Otherwise, if giving drops and there are no cash reserves, the church may have to turn to one or both of two options: securing a line of credit at a local bank or curtailing expenses further.

2. Weighted-Average Flexible Budget

In the weighted-average flexible budget, managers can go one step further and even assign a certain level of probability to each of the three projections. Obviously, this requires more research into past income patterns and a tighter internal accounting system.

The advantage, however, is that three separate, distinct projections are prepared. This in turn presents church leaders with options. The traditional method of budgeting usually results in belt-tightening when income drops. Often those reductions are across-the-board, which in many cases is either unfair or unjustified. Exhibit 5-4 is intended to illustrate how the figures for this budget type can be assembled in an understandable fashion.

These two types of flexible budgets are useful in different environments. The decision of which one to adopt depends on the complexity of the ministry, the sophistication of the accounting department, and the importance of the budget to the overall church goals.

The Zero-Based Budget

It has been well-established that once a church sets its goals for a specific period of time (usually a year), a budget then becomes an extension of that planning process. Finances become an indispensable resource in carrying out those goals.

However, where many churches have problems is in determining what is the best course of action when revenue begins to drop. The call usually goes out, "Cut the budget!" Often a reduction in spending is in line with the present demand to reduce expenses, but which expenses should the church cut? Which activities should be curtailed? Which employees need to have their hours cut back or even be laid off?

Most churches, when faced with this dilemma, try to be fair and equitable. This is because church boards and congregations, by and large, are governed by a majority rule standard, which, when translated, means a great deal of "give and take." The result is often a vote to either cut what is considered "fat" or an across-the-board reduction of expenses. This usually takes the form of a percentage cut in spending.

The major flaw in this approach is that it doesn't take into consideration the issue of the church's objectives or goals. That is to say, there needs to be an honest evaluation of specific departments and their contribution to the overall goals of the church. Unfortunately, in an effort to be fair, everyone suffers, or (as is the case with those ministries that are nonessential) some don't suffer but benefit. The benefit comes from the fact that they are considered important enough to be maintained right along with the missionaries, senior pastor's salary, and the utilities. Can every program or expense have equal importance and impact on the overall direction and goals of the church?

Zero-based budgeting (ZBB) avoids many of the common problems associated with the traditional budgeting approach. It permits an evaluation of current operations. Furthermore, it reduces the protection of a ministry simply because it exists, despite the fact that it may not be necessary. ZBB also eliminates the across-the-board budget cuts. Finally, it allows participation in the budgeting process by all department heads.

Since our discussion deals with churches, we will move away from the standard zero-based approach used by profit-oriented organizations. Instead, we will modify the ZBB concept to conform to the local church environment. However, the basic justification and principles behind this budgeting method remain the same; we will simply adapt them to the church environment.

Who's on First?

The first step in the zero-based budget process is for the board to determine which areas of the ministry are considered essential. In this prioritizing or ranking process, general overhead requirements need to be included.

For instance, if the church has a mortgage, the board cannot consider the debt as less important than funding a children's sports program. The reason is obvious: if it comes to cost cutting, you cannot set aside the mortgage in favor of the sports activities. Certain areas simply take priority even though they are not considered "pure ministry." The same would hold true with utilities, insurance, taxes, and what would be considered fixed expenses.

Therefore, in the process of placing priorities, the board needs to include those fixed expense areas as "packages" right along with a package of support for missions, youth, and other ministries.

What's in the Package?

To begin, packages or decision units need to be determined based on the priorities of the church. Package number one, due to its obvious importance, would be what business managers consider fixed expenses. They are mortgage/rent, utilities, taxes, insurance, basic phone service, and any other overhead item that is required to keep the church doors open.

Package number two would contain the basic compensation package of the senior pastor. Let's be honest here—without him in the pulpit each week, more than likely your offerings would drop. He is essential to the viability of the church.

But in certain cases, there may be some who say, no, it is the strong music program or the youth ministry that brings the people into the church. If that is the case, then the basic funding of that ministry moves to the second position.

Do you see what is happening here? The church is being broken down into operating units and then arranged by priority based on their contribution to the overall requirements and goals of the church. That is why basic costs are stressed instead of a single expense unit. That is, the phone bill is reduced to its lowest operational level in package number one. The pastor's compensation is reduced to salary and insurance but not added perks. We are after the lowest denominator in dealing with expenses.

Package number three may contain further administrative overhead items or a particular ministry area. Again, at the lower zero-based levels, we stick with the basics of the ministry with no frills or extras.

On it goes until you have all your annual projected budget broken down into packages and by priority.

Simply stated, the package should contain the following information:

- Who is the preparer, and what is the date of preparation?
- What is the purpose and description of activity or ministry?
- What is its cost, and what is the nature of all required resources?
- What are the expected benefits and results?
- What are the consequences if the activity is not funded?
- What is the recommended level at which the package should be funded?

Perhaps you have noticed by now that participation by your department heads or lay leaders involved in that ministry package is essential. If one person creates all the packages, you will not have one of the major budgeting principles in place—participation. If the budget is prepared "from on high" and set in place, the people operating within the framework of the budget will not be as committed to its success as they would be if they had a part in developing it. They would not "own" the budget and, therefore, would not have bought into the process of seeing that it works. (For sample budget package charts and worksheet, see Exhibits 5-5, 5-6, and 5-7.)

95

Ranking the Packages

Ultimately, some authoritative group will have to rank the packages by their priority. As unpopular as this may sound on the surface, down the road it will eliminate a lot of problems. It may be the Budget Committee who decides and then presents it to the church board. Depending on your church polity, it may end there, or it may be presented to the congregation for approval.

The primary issue is that you will be spending money as it becomes available on a monthly basis. If more money is available, then packages with lower priorities can be funded.

A question to consider at this point is, What if you just want to partially fund a program? Let's use the missions program as an example. Using this method of budgeting, missions can still receive a high priority. The important projects can receive money while the less crucial will be placed on the "back burner." Their budgets are tiered or divided into essential and less essential activities.

No doubt, the first two or three packages will be absolutely vital, with no anticipated cuts. However, it is advisable to divide the other ministries into sections, separating out the important from the "wish list" category. Thus, you have what could be called a modified zero-based budget.

True ZBB takes every cost, starts at a zero base and builds from that point. That may be a little too extreme for most churches because of their somewhat democratic way of making decisions. Much of what is decided in a church requires consensus, and the pure zero-based approach may not be that easy to explain or accept. It says that one ministry is more important than another.

However, by modifying the ZBB concept as I have described, you can actually fund *all* the ministries. It is the level *within* the ministries that can be adjusted.

Packages, therefore, are normally placed into three categories:

1. *Nondiscretionary and Legally Required Packages*. This group would more than likely be fully funded.

2. *Discretionary Packages*. This is always the largest group, and some of the ministries might have to be ranked. However, it is possible to place all current or essential ministries in this category. It needs to be understood though that there may be a time when the funds could run out, and certain projects within these packages will not be funded. Therefore, the items in the package need to be ranked to ensure money for the important items, followed by the less essential. (Again, do you see the importance of having the department heads involved in the budgeting process?)

3. *Wish List Packages*. This third group doesn't necessarily need to be ranked unless it is rather certain one or two of them will be funded, especially if it is necessary to make reductions later in the fiscal year. With the zero-based concept in place, it allows everyone to know what is going to happen because of the priority setting and ranking.

Summary

A successful zero-based program will increase the participation of all department heads in the budgeting process. This often encourages cost effectiveness, sometimes eliminates inefficiencies, and permits a great deal of flexibility in decision making. Church leaders are not tied down to a set annual budget with line-items firmly voted in place.

However, you need to know that zero-based budgeting demands more time and energy than conventional budgeting. Everyone involved will be forced to abandon traditional budgeting practices and accept an entirely different approach to resource allocation.

If you believe the zero-based concept is too drastic a change, you could adopt it the first year by assigning only a few packages. That is, use the conventional, straight-line, twelve-month budget but set the funding level slightly lower than full capacity. Then establish two or three packages at the "wish list" level. If funds are available, then money can be directed to these areas. It is possible to establish the ZBB program over a period of two or three years using this phase-in approach.

Zero-based budgeting is designed to make maximum use of the church's resources. Conventional budgeting, while easier to explain to the congregation and certainly simpler to administer, still assumes that previous budgets were valid and, therefore, a correct base to build upon.

A zero-based budget, on the other hand, says that each year the funding base begins at zero. Department heads and supervisors look at their own activities and say, "This is what I want to do, and this is how much it will cost." ZBB requires managers to also work from the ground up.

Keeping Your Finger on the Pulse

The annual budget should be reviewed on a regular, periodic basis. Usually, a monthly report of income and expense is used. Some ministries expand this information to show both a combined and individual department report. This combined statement depicts all the totals for a certain line-item. (See Exhibit 5-8.)

The departmental budget report shows income and expenses by department and by line-item. (See Exhibit 5-9.)

The accepted practice when preparing a more formalized report is to express the reporting periods as *Current* (the present accounting period) and *Year to Date* (activity for the months elapsed in the fiscal year). Most computerized accounting packages provide this information in their General Ledger modules under a monthly income statement.

On a quarterly basis, it is a good practice to measure revenue against expenses. (See Exhibit 5-10.) Simply determine a quarter's income versus expenses, with a variance (difference) comparison. Some managers like to see the dollar or percentage of income remaining in the unexpended portion of the budget.

Finally, at the end of the fiscal year, a summarized report of revenue and expense should be prepared. (See Exhibit 5-11.) This report ideally should be broken out by quarters. To simplify matters, a summary report of the budget line-items could be presented instead of a full report of all line-items. A more detailed report could be available for those who need this information. However, leaders on the church board would no doubt be satisfied with a simple summary report.

Conclusion

The advantage of an accurate, thorough budget results in effective planning, coordination, and control. The primary advantage of budgeting is that it forces managers to evaluate and think qualitatively about the overall ministry of the church, its strengths and weaknesses, and where it is headed or where it should be headed. By its very nature, budgeting requires leadership to identify problems and their possible solutions early in the budgeting process.

The process of budgeting mandates periodic review and revision of basic policies for the entire organization. The budget is often the single common thread weaving through the entire structure and ministry of the church.

Coordination of effort within the organizational structure is perhaps the primary reason most churches need a budget, whether leaders know it or not. Only when the actions of all the ministry departments are properly synchronized can an organization function efficiently.

Budgets are also a tool to help ensure that church resources are directed to the areas where they are needed. Optimum efficiency and balance of all aspects of a church are seldom possible. After all, it is essentially an "all-volunteer army." However, a carefully prepared budget will certainly minimize inefficiency and imbalance.

Once a current and meaningful budget is established, succeeding budgets will benefit by anticipating potential trouble spots and providing a framework for early solution.

The true success of a budget cannot and should not be measured by how close it comes to actual performance. A budget can also be effective by emphasizing the differences of projections from actual performance and by permitting critical analysis and study of those differences.

"Looking back" means a simple analysis of past giving patterns. Below is an example of a graph depiciting giving over a three-year period.

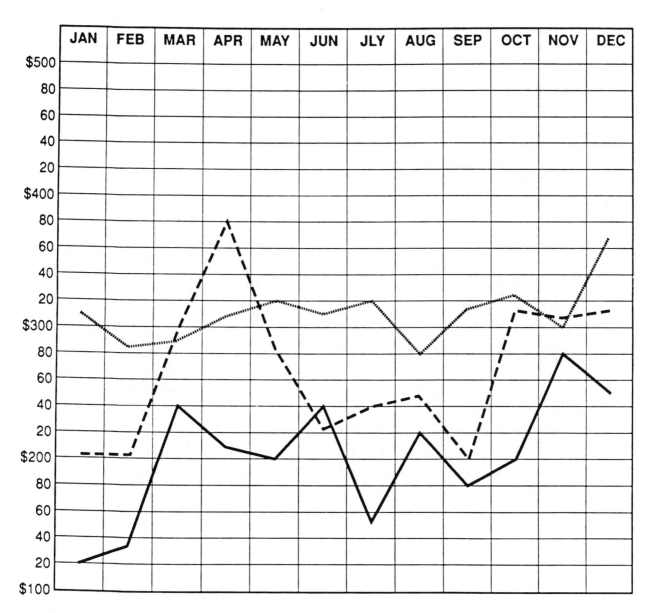

The analysis should show seasonal variations and other special fluctuations. The differences should be identified and understood.

1988 ——————— 1989 — — — — — 1990 ·················

Exhibit 5-1

STRAIGHT LINE BUDGET

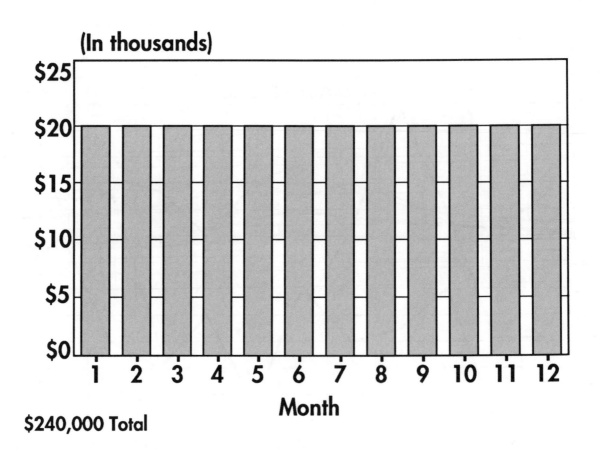

(In thousands)

$240,000 Total

Exhibit 5-2

AVERAGED BUDGET

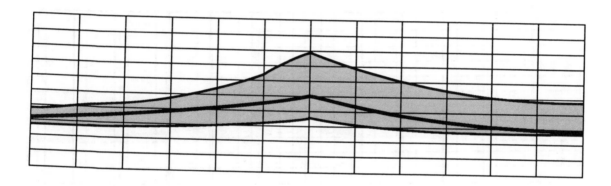

Exhibit 5-3

UNAVERAGED BUDGET

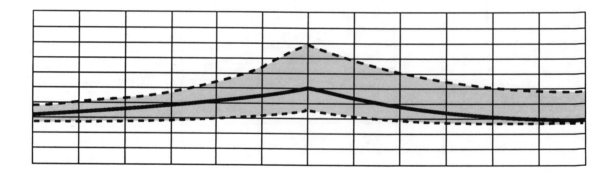

Exhibit 5-4

SAMPLE FUNDING

Zero Based Budget Packages
Allocation of Church Funds

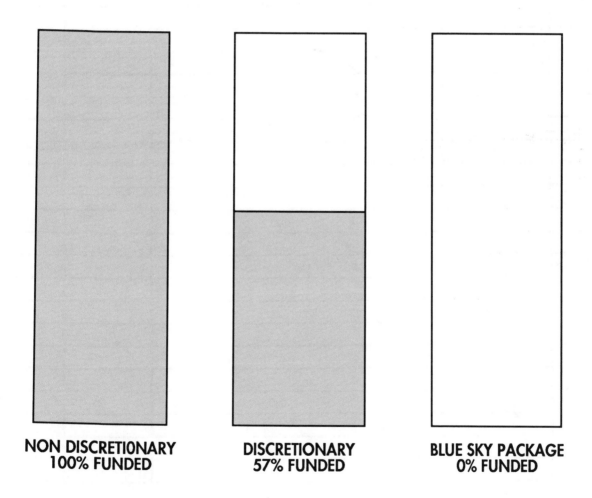

NON DISCRETIONARY
100% FUNDED

DISCRETIONARY
57% FUNDED

BLUE SKY PACKAGE
0% FUNDED

Exhibit 5-5

BUDGET PACKAGE

Fiscal Year 19____

Ministry/Activity: _____

Name of Preparer: _____

Date: _____

Key to Ranking: **A = Nondiscretionary**
B = Discretionary
C = Optional (wish list)

G/L #	Description	$ Amount	Ranking

Exhibit 5-6

BUDGET PACKAGE

Fiscal Year 19___

Ministry/Activity: _____

Name of Preparer: _____

Date: _____

Key to Ranking: A = Nondiscretionary
B = Discretionary
C = Optional (wish list)

G/L #	Description	$ Amount	Ranking
7010:0070	Salaries	To Be Determined	
7810:0070	Benefits	To Be Determined	
8410:0070	Supplies - Office	$200	B
8020:0070	Promotional Materials	$500	B
8372:0070	Non-Capital Equipment	$2000	C
8375:0070	Lease-Rental	$1500	B
8245:0070	Supplies - Music	$1000	A
8481:0070	Printing - Internal	$750	A/B
8480:0070	Printing - External	$750	B
8430:0070	Postage	$350	A
8374:0070	Maintenance - Equipment	$500	A
8400:0070	Supplies - Data Processing	$200	B
8420:0070	Books, Tapes, Subscriptions	$300	C
8645:0070	Purchased Services	$800	B
8665:0070	Special Activities	$500	B
8680:0070	Christmas Concert	$2200	A
8675:0070	Easter Concert (Special Music)	$2500	A
8670:0070	Retreats	$500	C
8690:0070	Food Service	$300	B
8660:0070	Seminars/Conferences	$500	B
8650:0070	Multimedia	$400	B

Exhibit 5-7

Summary of Expenses

	Current	Budget	$ Variance	% Var	Year-To-Date	Budget	$ Variance	% Var
Income								
Tithes and Offerings								
Tithes and Offerings	$113, 090	$118,035	($5,745)	(4.83)	$744,268	$713,012	$31,256	4.38
Catch Up Offering	0	0	0	0.00	0	0	0	0.00
Building Fund Offerings	40,315	56,667	(16,352)	(28.86)	250,089	340,000	(89,911)	(26.44)
Missions Project Offering	4,760	3,333	1,427	42.81	12,194	20,000	(7,806)	(39.03)
Deacons Fund Offering	462	833	(371)	(44.54)	4,898	5,000	(102)	(2.04)
Mission Project Sunday	0	0	0	0.00	0	0	0	0.00
Organ Fund	90	0	90	0.00	720	0	720	0.00
Teresa Memorial	0	0	0	0.00	0	0	0	0.00
Love Offerings	0	0	0	0.00	511	0	511	0.00
Misc. Dept. Offerings	0	0	0	0.00	0	0	0	0.00
Total Tithes & Offerings	158,717	179,668	(20.951)	(11.66)	1,012,680	1,078,012	(65,332)	(6.06)
Other Income								
Tape Ministry	331	0	331	0.00	1,575	0	1,575	0.00
Video Ministry	0	0	0	0.00	2,000	0	2,000	0.00
Daily Bread	45	0	45	0.00	41	0	41	0.00
Special Music Programs	0	0	0	0.00	(2,810)	0	(2,810)	(0.00)
Wedding Income	610	0	610	0.00	2,320	0	2,320	0.00
Awana Income	0	0	0	0.00	0	0	0	0.00
Total Other Income	10,834	4,340	6,494	149.63	85,012	26,048	58,964	226.37
Total Income	169,551	184,008	(14,457)	(7.86)	1,097,692	1,104,060	(6,368)	(0.58)
Transfer of Funds								
Deacon Fund Transfers	1,214	0	1,214	0.00	5,489	0	5,489	0.00
Love Offering Transfer	0	0	0	0.00	0	0	0	0.00
Miscellaneous Inc. Trns.	0	0	0	0.00	0	0	0	0.00
Total Transfer of Funds	1,214	0	1,214	0.00	5,489	0	5,489	0.00
General & Admin. Costs								
Cash (Over/Short)	0	0	0	0.00	0	0	0	0.00
Salaries	35,138	25,796	9,342	36.21	142,419	154,772	(12,353)	(7.98)
Non-Employee Compens.	20,505	14,937	5,568	37.28	86,104	89,618	(3,514)	(3.92)
Housing Allowance	19,807	14,249	5,558	39.01	78,278	85,496	(7,218)	(8.44)
Interest Income	0	0	0	0.00	0	0	0	0.00
Gain/Loss Sale Assets	0	0	0	0.00	0	0	0	0.00
Project Development	675	0	675	0.00	0	0	29,512	0.00
Amort. Exp. Bond Iss. Cost	0	0	0	0.00	0	0	0	0.00
Total G & A Costs	189,079	170,538	18,541	10.87	918,191	1,013,971	(95,780)	(9.45)
Net Income or Loss	($20,742)	$13,470	($34,212)	(253.99)	$174,012	$90,089	$83,923	93.16

Exhibit 5-8

Summary of Expenses

First Church
Departmental Statement of Operations
0054 - Jr. High School
Budget vs. Actual
for the six months ended June 30, 19___

	Current	Budget	$ Variance	% Var	Year-To-Date	Budget	$ Variance	% Var
Income								
Tithes and Offerings								
Missions Project Offering	$0	$0	$0	0.00	$0	$0	$0	0.00
Total Tithes & Offerings	0	0	0	0.00	0	0	0	0.00
Other Income								
Seminars & Conferences	0	0	0	0.00	0	0	0	0.00
Camps & Retreats	2,093	833	1,260	151.26	3,985	5,000	(1,015)	(20.30)
Special Activities	0	0	0	0.00	0	0	0	0.00
Missions Projects	12	0	12	0.00	52	0	52	0.00
Total Other Income	2,105	833	1,272	152.70	4,037	5,000	(963)	(19.26)
Total Income	2,105	833	1,272	152.70	4,037	5,000	(963)	(19.36)
Transfer of Funds								
Total Transfer of Funds	0	0	0	0.00	0	0	0	0.00
General & Admin. Costs								
Salaries	1,458	1,000	458	45.80	4,896	6,000	(1,104)	(18.40)
Non-Employee Compens.	137	92	45	48.91	549	553	(4)	(0.72)
Housing Allowance	375	249	126	50.60	1,500	1,496	4	0.27
Honorarium Travel & Exp.	0	21	(21)	(100.00)	0	124	(124)	(100.00)
Hon.-Speaking, Music, Other	0	0	0	0.00	0	0	0	0.00
Vacation Accural Adjmt.	0	0	0	0.00	0	0	0	0.00
FICA Tax Expense	94	0	94	0.00	352	0	352	0.00
Workers Compensation	0	20	(20)	(100.00)	0	120	(120)	(100.00)
Health Insurance	56	0	56	0.00	145	0	145	0.00
Life Insurance	0	16	(16)	(100.00)	25	98	(73)	(74.49)
Retirement Costs	0	0	0	0.00	0	0	0	0.00
Lease & Rental - Vehicle	0	0	0	0.00	0	0	0	0.00
Vehicle Cgs. Internal	0	0	0	0.00	0	0	0	0.00
Seminars & Conferences	0	13	(13)	(100.00)	0	75	(75)	(100.00)
Special Activities	0	50	(50)	(100.00)	0	300	(300)	(100.00)
Missions Project	42	8	34	425.00	84	52	32	61.54
Camps & Retreat	2,221	167	2,054	----.---	5,651	1,000	4,651	465.10
Food Service	0	0	0	0.00	0	0	0	0.00
Total G & A Costs	4,496	1,882	2,614	138.89	14,048	11,302	2,746	24.30
Net Income or Loss	($2,391)	($1,049)	($1,342)	(127.93)	($10,011)	($6,302)	($3,709)	(58.85)

Exhibit 5-9

FIRST CHURCH

Quarterly Budget Report

Three months ended March 31, 19___

	First Quarter Budget	First Quarter Actual	Variance Favorable (Unfavorable)	Unexpended Budget
REVENUE				
General Offerings	220,000	225,000	(5,000)	655,000
Building Fund	85,000	82,000	3,000	249,000
Missions Offerings	7,000	6,800	200	19,200
Special Projects	0	0	0	8,000
Misc. Income	1,000	1,200	(200)	11,800
TOTAL REVENUE	$313,000	$315,000	($2,000)	$943,000
EXPENSES				
Personnel Costs	147,900	147,500	400	444,100
Missions	15,000	14,550	450	45,450
General & Admin.	55,000	57,000	(2,000)	163,000
Building Expenses	82,000	83,000	(1,000)	245,000
TOTAL EXPENSE	$299,900	$302,050	($2,150)	$897,550

Exhibit 5-10

FIRST CHURCH

Revenue & Expense Budget FY 19___

	First Quarter	Second Quarter	Third Quarter	Fourth Quarter	Totals
REVENUES					
General Offerings	220,000	225,000	190,000	245,000	880,000
Building Fund	85,000	90,000	60,000	96,000	331,000
Missions Offering	7,000	6,000	5,900	8,000	26,900
Special Projects	0	5,000	0	3,000	8,000
Misc. Income	1,000	1,000	10,000	1,000	13,000
TOTAL REVENUES	313,000	327,000	265,900	353,000	1,258,900
EXPENSES					
Salaries	112,000	112,000	120,000	120,000	464,000
Benefits	20,500	20,000	20,500	20,500	82,000
Payroll Taxes	11,000	11,000	11,800	11,800	45,600
Missions Support	7,000	7,000	7,000	7,000	28,000
Honorariums	3,000	2,500	3,500	3,000	12,000
Utilities	6,000	4,500	7,000	4,000	21,500
Telephone	3,300	3,300	3,300	3,300	13,200
Promo/Advertising	1,500	1,500	1,500	1,500	6,000
Repairs/Maintenance	1,200	1,300	1,100	1,100	4,700
Curriculum/Books	1,200	200	3,000	500	4,900
Graphics/Printing	2,000	2,000	2,000	2,000	8,000
Maint. Contracts	3,000	3,000	3,000	3,000	12,000
Music Supplies	5,000	5,500	4,000	5,200	19,700
Office Supplies	625	625	625	625	2,500
Janitorial Supplies	675	675	675	675	2m700
Data Processing	2,000	2,000	2,000	2,000	8,000
Insurance	3,500	3,500	3,500	3,500	14,000
Depreciation	3,250	3,250	3,250	3,250	13,000
Travel/Entertain.	1,000	1,500	1,300	1,800	5,600
Mileage	3,000	3,000	2,000	3,500	11,500
Missions Projects	0	5,000	0	5,000	10,000
Camps/Retreats	2,000	1,500	10,000	1,500	15,000
Building Expenses	95,000	93,000	80,000	60,000	328,000
Professional Services	1,000	1,000	1,000	1,000	4,000
Food Service	3,600	4,000	2,500	5,000	15,100
Misc. Expense	5,000	5,000	5,000	5,000	20,000
TOTAL EXPENSE	297,350	298,350	299,550	275,750	1,171,000

Exhibit 5-11

Section 6

How to Turn Around a Financially Troubled Church

Every day it seems the phone rings with people wanting their bills paid. Donations aren't keeping up with expenses. And to make matters worse, two of your key staff people quit to take better paying jobs elsewhere.

Even the pastor's appeal letters have lost their appeal! They sound like they were written in a bomb shelter during an air raid. Every other word is underlined in red. The tone is urgent, more serious:"Send money now; we've got a major crisis here!"

Sound familiar? You may be trying to manage a church experiencing similar problems. These can be hard and discouraging times.

To begin with, we need to *identify* a financially troubled organization. This is necessary to prevent problems from occurring and to highlight those areas that may lead to further difficulties. What are the signs that a serious problem exists? Generally speaking, if two or more of the six questions listed below require a "yes" answer, you need to take a close look at your ministry's financial health. They are "red flags" that tell us something is wrong.

1. Is income from donations less this year than last year?
2. Is it necessary to withhold payroll occasionally due to lack of funds?
3. Are you behind in payments to your vendors more than sixty days?
4. Are you borrowing against a line of credit in order to pay operational expenses?
5. Are you delaying purchases of essential goods and services?
6. Are you holding off on needed repairs and maintenance?

There is no simple, quick-fix formula that always works to reverse these situations. However, there are a few proven principles and methods that can turn around a financially troubled ministry. Consider these points and think about how they apply to your church. Some of these recommendations may seem drastic, but there are, no doubt, churches today that are in all stages of difficulty. Some may be skirting the edge of trouble, while others are fighting for their very survival. (If your church is in neither of these positions, you might want to file this information away for future reference.)

A fundamental question ought to be asked at the outset of any discussion like this: Should this ministry even continue to stay in existence? That is, is it still fulfilling its mission statement? Perhaps the unthinkable should be examined—instead of a turn-around, maybe a shutdown is more appropriate. There is always the option of merging with another church, and this should be taken seriously. As unusual as it may seem, this is one way to keep the purpose of the ministry functioning and to maintain member friendship networks. A complete redirection or emphasis is another option that should be explored.

In the final analysis, these questions should be posed: Is this ministry still financially viable? Is it going to make it?

There are those organizations, however, that are experiencing an opposite problem— rapid growth. This can be just as troublesome if not managed properly. You can end up building and staffing for explosive, temporary growth and then experience some painful cutbacks and layoffs down the road. Many major churches in the country have gone through some rather severe reductions as a result of a period of fast growth followed by declining revenues.

Before considering some of the specific measures required to hold off a further financial decline, review some of the primary characteristics of a nonprofit organization. This is important because it sets down some basic guidelines and philosophy.

The term *nonprofit*, when it is applied to an organization, conjures up different meanings to different people. Richard Wacht in his book *Financial Management in Nonprofit Organizations* points out that, for some people, *nonprofit* may mean "charitable, tax-exempt, publicly owned, or a prohibition against 'making money' from operations."[11]

Nonprofit organizations originally got their names because their operations were for the most part guided by motives other than monetary gain, or "profit." However, in general this title has tended to confer a significant misunderstanding concerning their operation among outsiders and, surprisingly, even among their own managers, especially those people who are appointed or elected to their governing bodies.

For example, many church boards would have a difficult time with their church ending a fiscal year with a surplus—they want the church to break even. They believe nonprofit means just that—no operating cash surplus. The fact of the matter is, generating cash surpluses may be the only way a certain church can survive and expand its base and ability to function effectively.

11. Richard F. Wacht, *Financial Management in Nonprofit Organizations* (Georgia State U. Business Publication, 1984), p. 20.

As Wacht explains, "An organization must be financially solvent and maintain adequate liquidity in order to continue to operate; hence, it should, to whatever extent its governing board chooses, support itself out of operating cash surpluses."[12] It is at this point that many Christian organizations get into trouble. The practice of not having adequate cash reserves both to meet emergencies and to grow isn't given a high priority.

There is a second major reason churches have financial difficulties. It involves the leadership structure. Most churches philosophically operate with a *dual* "management structure." That is because their very nature and survival relies on simultaneously achieving two distinct objectives.

The first goal could be called a *professional* goal. For example, a mission organization generally exists to recruit, train, and send workers. A church is called to reach and make disciples of all men. You could call these public or professional goals.

A second type of goal for a church is to set forth *financial* objectives that are designed to meet the *professional* objectives. Without proper financial planning and control to ensure that cash is available to support the public goals, even the most high-sounding, worthy purposes will fail.

These two sets of goals must be met simultaneously—that is, one cannot take precedence over the other. And it is at this exact point that many organizations, especially churches, have difficulty. I call this a conflict between the "visionaries" and the "bottom-liners." If either mind set prevails, the effectiveness of the organization will suffer.

One fundamental fact remains. It is a lot easier to raise funds when you can point to a record of professional success coupled with a good track record of fiscal responsibility.

When a church extends itself beyond its capability to meet its obligations, it may be viewed by the public as inefficient, or tolerant of poor management. That impression then translates into a drop in donations, which results in cash flow problems.

A professionally well-conceived program that fails to have good financial planning will produce the same result as a well-financed but poorly conceived professional program. The net effect is that the public will withhold its giving. Let's examine some of the specific steps that could be taken to eliminate some of the "red flags" mentioned earlier.

Maintain Credibility

The key word here is *integrity*. First, you want credibility with your donors, next with your suppliers, and then with your employees. Ask yourself and your key people three things:

12. Ibid., p. 20.

"How do we represent ourselves to the public, to our suppliers, and to our employees?"

"Do people perceive us in a positive light?"

"What do people reasonably expect of our ministry?"

If you make promises to your donors, suppliers, or employees, you absolutely must deliver on them. Otherwise, your credibility will slip at an increasingly faster rate.

Control the Flow

You don't need to be a rocket scientist to figure out that cash flow is a major factor in the health of an organization. Herb Adler may have said it all: "Happiness is positive cash flow." For our purposes, it isn't simply happiness we want but *survival*. Survival is positive cash flow!

Time is not necessarily on your side in a cash-poor situation—therefore, certain steps need to be taken to accelerate a positive response. What I mean by this is that you need to move fast to close the payables versus receivables shortfall.

The treasurer or financial officer should have hands-on involvement with payables. He needs to allocate the limited financial resources available to him. We have a Christian moral responsibility to pay what we owe. The first priority is to make payroll, utilities, and rent. Perhaps you are forced to deal with new suppliers, which may mean you are on a COD basis. These need to be paid as well.

One person, the highest finance officer, should personally review the payables. Make partial payments to those vendors that fall within the following profile:

- Provider of vital goods or services
- "Wolf at the Door"—a vendor who is threatening to "blow your house down" with threats of aggressive collection proceedings
- Vendors whose survival is being threatened by late payments and who can't make payroll because your church owes them so much

Another strategy is to examine those ministries or departments that are at best marginal. Some may no longer be functioning in the best interests of the church. You may have what's called a "cash cow"—a ministry or department that consumes a lot of cash but doesn't give very much "milk" in return. If so, it may be time to switch cows.

Freeze Hiring

No one is added to the staff or replaced at this point. This may mean that job descriptions get changed and that some people will have to hold dual positions. It may also be necessary to cut hours. The point of such drastic steps is that you absolutely must gain control over your cash resources and spending.

Get Usable Information

This is important. Examine the information being provided from various departments.

- Accounting information needs to be timely.
- Donor records should be accurate, with up-to-date postings.
- If leaders get a lot of reports that they really don't need or have time to read, stop having them prepared.
- Also, have some of the reports prepared in summary format rather than with a lot of supporting detail data.

Quite simply, the information must have a use and be accurate. Otherwise, it is not needed. Also, if the data isn't trustworthy, take whatever steps are necessary to improve it.

Communicate the Situation to Employees

"I've got good and bad news," the pilot reported over the loudspeaker. "The bad news is we've been lost for over an hour. But the good news is that, due to a strong tail wind, we're really making good time." Is that the situation your church faces? If so, deal with the bad news right away.

Call a meeting of the key leaders, department heads, and whoever else needs to attend. Explain to them the problems the church is having. Then ask them to tell you the best and worst aspects of the church. Let them vent their opinions—but *listen*! Listen for the general morale level. Listen to those people who are outspoken, both the positive and the negative people. Ask them what they would do if they were in your position right now. Ask them what it is this ministry does best. Then repeat back those positive points the people just voiced. Point out the positive—highlight it, emphasize it! Then never look back or bring up the negative again.

Next, call a meeting of the rest of the employees. Recite to them some of the bad reports you've heard and then move on to the positive characteristics of the church. Tell them some good news! This should be followed by a time to encourage the staff to submit their suggestions on how things can be turned around.

Adopt a Motto

Develop a slogan or motto—something upbeat and, again, positive.

A good example is the story of Doolittle's Tokyo raid during World War II. Jimmy Doolittle trained a hand-picked group of pilots to fly B-25 bombers off the deck of an aircraft carrier—something totally unheard of until then. These brave men flew the bombers to Japan and bombed Tokyo. The actual damage wasn't nearly as significant as the psychological effect on the Japanese people, not to mention the effect on the American soldier's morale. Tokyo, the capital city and the home of the emperor, had been bombed by the enemy. Jimmy Doolittle got a lot of "bang for his buck"! The point of this illustration is that you need to find some type of psychological lift for your church.

Consider a Change in Image

Take a good look at your church's logo. When was the last time it was changed or modernized? Perhaps the stationery needs a face lift. Also, have the receptionists answer the telephones with a different greeting.

Suggest that someone other than the pastor communicate financial needs to the congregation.

Why not ask the chairman of the board of the church to write and sign the next appeal letter?

Pick a specific, successful ministry or activity within your professional area and focus attention on it. Let your donors know what you are doing in a positive light—give them some good news.

We want to project a new, fresh image and not a picture of an organization with serious financial problems.

Develop an Action Plan

It's been said many times, but it's worth repeating: "Fail to plan—plan to fail." Most successful ministries have some form of strategic planning. At the minimum, this may consist of an annual operating plan consisting of projected income statements, balance sheets, cash-flow statements, capital budgets, and supporting schedules. Churches that have developed their planning process further include some sort of long-range plan.

Aside from the obvious fact that we want to get the church out of financial trouble, there are basically three major reasons for preparing an action plan:

1. Benefits are derived from the actual planning activity itself.
2. The plan provides a basis for measuring actual financial results against projections.
3. The plan acts as a vehicle for communicating to others what it is the ministry is trying to accomplish.

If the "red flags" mentioned earlier are present in your organization, a short-term plan needs to be developed. You can't just sit back in a reactive mode and allow the next crisis to hit. A game plan should be set forth to begin the turnaround process. What if giving drops another 5 percent? What if giving increases 10 percent? What is the first and second action you should take in response?

Furthermore, it is healthy to be forced to put down on paper where the ministry is in terms of what it has to offer, its donor base, and its relative "competitive" position in the donor market. Perhaps you may think that being competitive is unspiritual. But the facts are that your base of donor support has other ministries and appeals competing for its dollars. Local churches can suffer because of appeals from mission agencies, TV and radio ministries, and other Christian organizations. It isn't right, but it still happens. Church members should support these organizations out of "over and above" giving, but realistically it doesn't always happen that way.

Also, the ministry's financial requirements and the resources needed are important. It's possible to use what's called a "break even chart." It's important to determine how much money it takes to keep an organization alive. You might want to do a little research into how one of these charts is prepared and what it could show you. A short-term action plan is a must for a church in need of a turnaround.

Generate New Cash

A. Sell Assets

This is the most bitter pill of all to swallow. Having to cut back can be viewed as God removing His blessing from your church. But who does the ministry belong to? Are you the owner of the organization or simply the manager? How you answer those questions will determine whether you are willing to let go of those things that are no longer necessary to the life of the ministry.

Depending on how serious the condition, you need to do whatever is necessary to save the ministry. There are many reasons why God may want the work to be smaller—the greatest of which may be because you or your board want it to be big. Think about it!

Assets may include equipment, buildings, vehicles, computers—whatever isn't absolutely vital to the ministry may have to be sold.

B. Reduce Inventories

Next, you need to start to squeeze or cut inventories of supplies. This means reorder points should be reduced. I knew of one church that ordered large amounts of paper goods because they felt the suppliers would eventually cut them off for slow payment.

First of all, as a church, you really shouldn't buy something without a sure way of paying for it. That isn't the biblical model. Second, if the supplier is vital to your ministry, why destroy the relationship? Order in smaller quantities so you can pay the supplier more often. This will keep a better flow of materials and save a supplier from refusing to deal with you.

It also might be necessary to identify those items that are hardly used and eliminate them from the inventory.

C. Collect Your Receivables

Another obvious way to generate cash is to collect your receivables. For those of you involved in managing churches, the term *receivables* may sound like something only businesses have to contend with. However, a church might have two areas that could be considered receivables. If a pledge program is used, the people should be encouraged in a tasteful and sensitive way to be consistent with their financial commitments.

If the church has a day school, unpaid tuition is a receivable. Consider sending out a statement each month. Also, an interest charge on unpaid balances is appropriate here. Use some compassion though, for there are single mothers and others who have genuine financial struggles of their own. If you adopt a late-penalty procedure, the parents should have thirty to forty-five days advance notice of this new policy. The monthly statements should then be aged in thirty-day increments.

A school also needs to have a written policy on how to handle delinquent accounts. Again, mail it to all parents with an appropriate amount of lead time.

If your ministry bills for goods and services, a standard accounts receivable collections procedure should be established. This would include delinquent notices that go out in a regular, periodic fashion.

Get Some Help

One final suggestion is to seek outside help. None of us have all the answers. Furthermore, lack of time often doesn't allow the luxury to reinvent the wheel. You don't want to repeat mistakes or go off on paths that could, in the long run, make matters worse.

There are fine Christian organizations and individuals throughout the country that could offer help. At a minimum, get a good accountant involved so you will get a clear perspective on the financial picture.

Experts are available in areas of fund-raising, organizational management, data processing, and so forth. Call them, tell them your situation, and don't be afraid to ask them how much it would cost for their services.

In conclusion, turning around a financially troubled ministry is no easy task. You will need complete cooperation from the senior pastor, the leadership of the church, and the employees of the ministry. Everyone should know that they may need to make some sacrifices. Also, many of the philosophies and methods of the past may need changing. Cooperation and flexibility are the key words. Without these, no turnaround will take place, and the church will be back where it was—only in deeper trouble.

Further, keep in mind that once a ministry is restored to a healthy footing, it needs to stay there. Hopefully, whatever caused the problems in the first place has been identified and dealt with.

The next step, however, is to prevent it from recurring in the future. That is where the action plan referred to earlier comes into play. It's time to switch from a short-term mode to a more long-range outlook. That means more than just making plans for the future. It also involves putting in place internal controls and checkpoints that will identify those "red flags" before they make it to the top of the flag pole.

Churches having financial problems do little to advance the cause of Christ. The entire tone and direction of the ministry, as well as the testimony to the outside community, suffers. Churches owe it to their suppliers, employees, and donors—and, above all, they owe it to Christ—to keep their ministries headed in the right direction.

Workers Worthy of Hire

I t is not uncommon for a church today to spend at least 50 percent of its total annual budget on staff salaries. Furthermore, the total cost of employee compensation includes more than just the dollars spent on salaries. Other expenditures such as health and life insurance, workers compensation, Social Security taxes, disability insurance, and retirement programs should be figured into the equation. When the total employee costs are calculated, it represents a major share of the church budget.

Yet, this is an area where many churches have difficulty. With that much money at stake, one would think that policies and reasonable practices would be set in place. But that is not always the case. It often isn't so much a problem of intent or neglect; it is simply not knowing what to do. Though Scripture says "the laborer is worthy of his hire" (1 Timothy 5:18), it gets a little more complicated than that in today's society. Which laborers, under what conditions, full-time or part-time, exempt or nonexempt?

The whole field of personnel management has undergone so many changes in recent years that the business world has even given it a new name—Human Resources Development. Although the principle of a laborer being worthy of his wages is true (Matthew 10:10), we need more specifics in dealing with church employees today.

Stewardship of financial resources extends from its beginning in the church member's pocket (actually it starts in the hand of God) to the manner in which the church staff is compensated. This flow of funds, however, requires some accountability, organization, and structure.

The initial step in this process should be the forming of a small group that, for lack of a better title, could be called the personnel committee. The function of this group is to set personnel policies, establish and administer an equitable compensation program, and act as a sounding board and a last resort in dealing with employee related problems. The pastor could serve on this committee, but the rest of the group should be laypeople. This will ensure objectivity and openness.

The members of the personnel committee, under the authority of the church's ruling board, would be responsible for finding, interviewing, and recommending what, in their opinion, would be acceptable individuals for all paid staff positions. The exception would be the locating and recommendation of a senior pastor. Their duties would include the following:

1. Study the needs for future personnel.
2. Develop and accurately adjust on an ongoing basis all position descriptions.
3. Develop and maintain an organization chart and personnel policy.
4. Locate, interview, and recommend to the church all employed staff personnel.
5. Recommend to the board the salary and benefit program.[13]

The personnel committee serves a vital role in the church. It has a significant part in determining how a large proportion of the church budget will be spent each year. These people need to be mature and sensitive, firm but fair in their deliberations.

Personnel Policy

Even if a church has only one employee—the senior pastor—it needs to have a policy relating to employment. Usually, as a church grows in size, the size of the staff grows with it. Personnel policies out of necessity also tend to grow in a corresponding fashion. The larger church will have a need to maintain organizational structure and avoid legal problems associated with employees. A small church simply needs to have in writing the basics of an employment policy.

Sample Personnel Policy Manual

Generally speaking, most personnel policies follow a standard format. Although the sample policy provided here may seem too complicated or appear to be directed toward a larger church and therefore inapplicable for small churches, simply use those portions that relate your own church situation while discarding those that don't apply.

13. Mark Short, *Church Administration Handbook*, ed. Bruce Powers (Nashville: Broadman, 1985), p. 82.

PERSONNEL POLICY MANUAL
FIRST CHRISTIAN CHURCH OF LAKE CITY

Introductory Statement

Welcome to First Christian Church. We trust you will enjoy your work here and that we will be proud of you as a member of our staff.

In this booklet, we explain what the Church expects from you and what you can expect from the Church. We have tried to use simple, clear language to avoid misunderstandings. If any statement in this booklet is not clear to you, please feel free to ask questions.

We try to be careful to hire only those persons we feel reasonably sure are qualified to do the work of the Lord and who will be congenial with others working here. If we hire someone who will not or cannot do the work satisfactorily, it will be necessary to discharge him or her to permit the Church to fulfill its mission to serve Christ and our people.

We hope that you will find satisfaction in your work. May we both enjoy pleasant relations for many years.

This handbook puts into writing, in the same manner as a contract, what you can expect from First Christian Church and what is expected from you. We want you to call to our attention anything you feel is not right.

Classification of Employees

Pastoral Staff
Individuals who are responsible for major ministry responsibilities.

General Employees
Full-time personnel employed in support functions or as ministry directors. *Full-time* is defined as a permanent employee working a minimum of thirty-two hours per week.

First Christian Church uses the following terms as a basis for its payroll system and personnel administration:

Salaried Employees (Exempt)

Personnel paid on the basis of an annual salary and not subject to premium pay for overtime.

Hourly Employees (Nonexempt)

Personnel paid on the basis of an hourly rate and subject to premium pay for overtime. Hourly employees are full-time or part-time personnel.

Temporary Hourly Employee

An individual whose service is for a brief period of time. He or she may work part time, a regular forty-hour week, or be on call.

Evaluation Period

During the first ninety days of employment, each new staff member will meet several times with his or her direct supervisor for the purpose of monitoring job performance. At the end of this period, a formal performance appraisal will be discussed. Subsequently, you will receive a formal performance evaluation annually on your hire date anniversary.

Attendance

Every employee is expected to work all his or her scheduled hours, to report for work on time, and to work the end of the work period.

If, for any reason, you cannot report for work on time, telephone the Church as far in advance of your starting time as possible. State why you will be absent and how long you expect to remain absent or late.

Absence for three consecutive work days without notification is considered job abandonment. Absence without approval is considered unexcused and will be subject to discipline.

An employee may be tardy three times per month before the Church will consider discharge or discipline due to habitual tardiness.

Change of Employee Status

Notify the church at once whenever there is a change in your

- Address
- Telephone number
- Person to notify in case of emergency, accident, or illness
- Name or marital status
- Number of dependents
- Insurance beneficiary

Group Insurance Program

Group insurance is offered as a part of the Church's benefit program for full-time employees. For the purposes of definition and unless otherwise approved, all provisions of the employee benefit program apply to full-time employees only. *Full-time*, for insurance purposes, is interpreted to mean thirty-two hours or more per week.

A brochure is available that outlines all the health and life insurance benefits available to full-time employees.

The cost of the insurance for you as an employee will be paid for by the Church.

Vacation Benefit

Vacations will be granted, with pay, to all full-time employees after one (1) year of continuous employment in the Church. The following conditions prevail:

1. Vacations may be accumulated up to a maximum of twenty (20) working days. Accrued vacation days may be carried from one twelve-month period to the next, up to a maximum of twenty (20) working days.

2. The amount of vacation granted will be on the basis of unbroken service with the Church.

3. Pay will not be given in lieu of unused vacation.

4. Employees who have worked less than one year but more than six (6) months can be entitled to pro-rated vacation time at the discretion of the appropriate supervisor.

5. Employees who resign from First Christian Church with proper advance notification (notice in writing two weeks prior to termination) and have completed one or more years of service will be entitled to earned vacation pay at the time of termination.

6. Employees who resign without giving proper notice, or who are discharged for cause, shall not be entitled to earned vacation pay.

Employees—Exempt and Nonexempt

All full-time employees shall be granted vacations based on tenure of employed service in the Church in accordance with the following services:

One (1) year and less than five (5) years	2 weeks
Six (6) years and less than ten (10) years	3 weeks
Eleven plus (11 +) years	4 weeks

Pastoral Staff

Additional absences may be supported for local work at camps, tours, seminars, crusades, or conferences according to full-time maximums. All pay received in excess of expenses will be given to the church payroll officer.

Staff

First year	2 weeks
2-5 years of service	3 weeks
6-10 years of service	4 weeks
11-15 years of service	5 weeks

Pastor Advisory Level

1-5 years	4 weeks
6 years plus	5 weeks

Senior Pastor

1-5 years	4 weeks
(plus 2 weeks for outside meetings)	
6 years plus	5 weeks

Employees—Temporary

No paid vacation

Holidays

All full-time employees shall be granted the following ten (10) paid holidays per year.

New Year's Eve (1/2 day)

New Year's Day

Good Friday (1/2 day)

Memorial Day

Independence Day

Labor Day

Thanksgiving Day and the Friday following

Christmas Eve

Christmas Day

Floating holiday (to be designated by the employee)

Those full-time employees who are required to work on one of the designated holidays shall be granted compensatory time off.

If a holiday falls on a Saturday, it will be observed on the preceding Friday, and if it falls on a Sunday, it will be observed the following Monday.

Sick Leave

Temporary employees and those working less than thirty-two (32) hours per week are not eligible for sick leave. Paid sick leave is granted to the following employees after six (6) months' service:

Sick leave shall accrue from the date of hire at the rate of seven (7) hours per month to a maximum of 120 hours. Employees starting from the first through the fifteenth of the month will accrue seven (7) hours for that month; employees starting the sixteenth through the end of the month will accrue three and a half (3 1/2) hours for that month and seven (7) hours per month thereafter until the maximum is reached.

Accrued sick days may be carried over from one twelve-month period to the next up to a maximum of 120 hours in any twelve-month period.

Paid sick leave is to be used exclusively for the employee's personal illness, immediate family illness, or medical appointment.

Temporary or Part-time Employees: No paid sick leave.

Pay Periods

Paychecks are issued on the 15th and last day of each month. When payday falls on a Saturday or Sunday or a public holiday, paychecks will usually be issued on the preceding work day.

Hours and Attendance

The normal work day is from 8:15 A.M. to 5:15 P.M.

The work week is from Monday through Friday for a total of forty (40) hours.

Variations in the hours for work may be made. Where work schedules may require it, a staggering of hours for the establishment of separate work shifts is sometimes made.

Leave of Absence

A leave of absence without pay will be considered for extraordinary circumstances not detrimental to the ministry of your department. This can be granted only at the option of the person who supervises that department and must be approved by the appropriate supervisor and the Church Administrator.

Lunch and Rest Periods

The amount of time for the lunch period is one (1) hour. A coffee break of fifteen (15) minutes in the morning and fifteen (15) minutes in the afternoon is also allowed.

Jury Duty

Employees who are required to be absent from work for jury duty will be paid the money they would have earned had they worked their normal work schedule. Any fee received for jury duty shall be turned over to the Church. If jury pay exceeds normal Church pay, the employee may keep the jury pay in excess of Church pay.

Expenses and Allowance

Expenses incurred while on Church business by any employee shall be recognized for reimbursement, if authorized in advance and approved by the appropriate authority.

Conference Attendance and Graduate Study

The Church provides a program of subsidized conference attendance and graduate study for all full-time, salaried, exempt personnel, provided that the conferences and training are related to work performed by the employee. Amount of subsidy is subject to budget provisions and approval of the Chairman of the Board or his designee. The provision does not alter hours and attendance requirements.

Exempt staff have the opportunity to enroll in graduate courses offered by colleges in the community, provided that:

A. The courses have a direct relationship to the work of the Church

B. Only one course shall be taken at a time

C. Approval is given by the Chairman of the Board or his designee prior to the beginning of the course

First Christian Church will reimburse tuition for approved courses after verification of course completion has been submitted to the employee's personnel file indicating a passing grade.

Grievances

Employees are expected to discuss grievances with their immediate supervisor. If the matter cannot be settled, the grievance shall be discussed with the employee and the employee's immediate supervisor by the Senior Pastor. If the employee is then not satisfied with the settlement, the employee may present, in writing, the issue in question to the ruling board to be further reviewed.

Dismissal

Any employee may be discharged at any time for cause. No nonexempt employee will be discharged without the prior approval of the ruling board. In all cases, the employee shall be entitled to know the reasons for the dismissal.

Dress Code

In carrying out the Lord's work, you will likely come into contact with many visitors, parents of students, and members of the congregation. As your work will be under constant observation by these visitors, it is necessary to present as favorable an appearance as possible. You are requested to dress appropriately at all times in light of Whom we represent.

You should be well-groomed, presenting a favorable appearance that is appropriate to the service you are providing.

Voluntary Employment

Employment at First Christian Church of Lake City is voluntary, and at-will. This means that the employee is free to leave the Church's employment at any time by giving reasonable notice, and the Church is free to discharge the employee at any time by giving reasonable notice. The Church does not need cause to discharge any employee; the employee serves at-will of the employer.

Code of Conduct

First Christian Church of Lake City is an evangelical church. It bases its teachings and guidelines for lifestyle and work ethics on the teachings found in the New Testament Scriptures. We expect the employee's conduct, on the job as well as off the job, to be in line with the moral, spiritual, and ethical guidelines of the Scriptures.

Violations of these principles can result in termination of employment.

Job Descriptions

Each staff person should have a written job description outlining his or her basic responsibilities and duties. The personnel committee should be the group that identifies the positions and prepares the position profiles. The importance of job descriptions cannot be overemphasized. An employee has the right to know what is expected of him regarding his job duties, where he fits on the organization chart and who, if anyone, he is supposed to supervise.

The content of the job description will depend for the most part on the specific job itself. First and foremost, the description should focus on the job position and not on the individual filling the job. Job descriptions should also be somewhat flexible. Conditions and circumstances change, and therefore the job description should change as well. It is a standard or guide—not rules set in stone.

The job description is also a valuable tool in evaluating employees. This subject will be dealt with later in this chapter.

The following is a sample list of church job descriptions. For the sake of flexibility and the need to be applicable across a broad range of church sizes and staffing situations, specific, individual duties have been omitted.

Senior Pastor

Responsible for all activities of the church. Responsibilities regularly include conducting services, making visitations, performing special ceremonies (such as weddings or funerals), counseling, leading business meetings, and overseeing the work of other church staff members.

Executive Pastor

Shares the responsibility for church activities with, and is responsible to, the senior pastor. Typically manages the professional staff on behalf of or in the absence of the senior pastor. On occasion acts as liaison with the lay leadership of the church. May be called upon to assist in all church functions or assigned specific areas of responsibility.

Assistant Pastor

Assists in one or more church ministries as delegated by the senior or executive pastor. May be assigned a specific area or called upon to serve in all areas.

Pastor to Singles

Responsible for the functions related to a singles ministry. Plans and directs meetings, outings, and special occasions. Counsels singles and trains leaders as needed.

Pastor/Director of Children's Ministries

Responsible for the functions related to children, usually focusing on grade-school-age children. Plans and directs activities, trains teachers, purchases supplies, and meets with parents for counseling.

Pastor of Care and Growth

Responsible for those areas related to pastoral care, which include but are not limited to visitation, weddings, and funerals. Provides oversight to volunteers involved in church visitation.

Pastor of Missions and Outreach

Direct, administer, and coordinate missions and outreach programs to integrate into each member and regular attender a mind-set for ministry and outreach beyond church family. Provides leadership by effectively managing the ministries of missions, community outreach, and evangelism. To develop and maintain "world Christian" perspective among members. Develop special programs of outreach. Assist minister of music in developing and maintaining the medium of music as an evangelistic outreach to the community.

Youth Director

Responsible for the functions related to youth, which are typically junior and senior high school age. Plans and directs activities, outings, special occasions, and youth worship services. Counsels youth and trains helpers as needed.

Christian Education Director

Responsible for planning and implementing the Christian education program, usually focusing on birth through grade-school-age children. Establishes curriculum, trains teachers, purchases supplies, and meets with parents for counseling. Attends seminars. May also include responsibility for youth and adults where appropriate for coordination.

Minister of Music

Responsible for the music activities of the church. Establishes choirs, selects and trains choir members, and selects music. Works with senior pastor in programming for regular and special church services. Typically responsible to lead worship for church services. Responsible to obtain organist and piano accompanist. Plans and conducts special music events.

Church Business Administrator

Responsible for the business activities of the church. Has oversight for operations, general office, finance, properties, and insurance. Establishes personnel and operations policies. Responsible for administrative records.

Organist/Pianist

Responsible for playing for any or all worship services, weddings, memorial services, funerals, choir rehearsal, and performances/concerts. Work for, or closely with, the minister of music. May be part of worship committee to plan worship services.

Sound Technician

Responsible for set-up and maintenance of all sound and duplicating equipment during scheduled activities.

Secretary—Junior

Performs routine secretarial duties. May take and transcribe dictation. Types letters and reports, answers phone, makes appointments, files documents. This is the lowest secretarial level.

Secretary—Senior

Performs moderately complex secretarial duties for senior-level manager or executive. Typically takes and transcribes dictation. Sets up and administers filing systems, types normal and confidential documents, prepares reports, arranges meetings and appointment schedules, receives and answers mail, provides direction to lower-level clerical employees, and assists in developing office policies and procedures. This is the highest secretarial level below the executive secretary.

Receptionist

Receives and greets customers and other callers and directs them to appropriate department. Operates a switchboard by receiving and placing local and long-distance calls. Performs typing and other clerical work as directed.

Janitor

Cleans and maintains buildings and offices by sweeping, dusting, polishing, scrubbing, mopping, and waxing. Removes trash, cleans furniture, washes windows, waxes and buffs floors, cleans carpets, and performs other necessary maintenance to keep the facilities clean and orderly.

Groundskeeper/Gardener General Maintenance

Responsible for maintenance of property grounds and equipment, including mowing, watering, and replacement. May be under the supervision of the building maintenance senior or supervisor.

Preschool Director

Teaches preschool children, supervises teachers, schedules school activities and field trips, schedules employees, and may perform some bookkeeping functions.

Early Childhood Coordinator

Oversees preschool and nursery/toddler programs. Assists children's pastor in recruiting preschool teachers and leaders. Offers ongoing training, support, and discipleship of preschool teachers. Supervises preschool assistant and nursery-/toddler staff. Attends weekly and monthly staff and committee meetings. Evaluates ongoing programs and strategies for improvement. Orders and oversees curriculum, equipment, and supplies, and oversees facility care and maintenance.

Elementary Teacher

Teaches children in elementary classes, does lesson plans, prepares bulletin board, coordinates field trips, leads class in light singing, and handles light telephone responsibilities.

High School Teacher

Gives specialized teaching in a given subject area and teaches in a secondary area. Responsibilities include, but are not limited to, lesson plans, extracurricular activities, counseling, and serving on departmental committees.

School Principal

The school principal is responsible for overall administration of the school. The areas of responsibility include, but are not limited to, the development of policies and the oversight of office administration, teachers, curriculum, student discipline, finance, and other duties as directed by the proper ruling body.[14]

14. "Ministry Salary Survey," Christian Management Association, Diamond Bar, Calif., 1991.

A blank job description form (Exhibit 7-1) is provided at the end of this chapter. The sample form is a model for a medium to large church—although it can be adapted for a smaller organization.

Evaluating the Staff

One area that seems to cause some disagreement in churches has to do with the reviewing of employee performance, especially when it relates to pastoral staff. Without going into the arguments on both sides of the issue, it has been shown that some sort of ongoing and adequate staff evaluation from top to bottom will yield positive results. There are two main points to keep in mind here: accountability and effectiveness.

At the risk of appearing as though the church is being run like a secular corporation, there are certain aspects of corporate practice that could certainly be implemented in the local church. Simply stated, it is neither good stewardship nor common sense to simply give church employees raises every year, especially merit increases above a Cost of Living Adjustment (COLA), without some tie-in to effectiveness. On the other hand, if a church does correlate raises to performance, how is that done? You wouldn't want to link the pastor's salary to the number of baptisms or the bookkeeper's pay check to positive cash flow!

By way of principle, church leaders should certainly have an understanding and grasp of what they can expect from their staff. On the other hand, the church staff deserves certain courtesies from their employer—the church. While not even pretending to be exhaustive, the following guidelines offer a philosophy or overview of how church leaders should view their staff.

1. *The principle of work assignments commensurate to capacity and interest.* Every employee's potential should be given consideration in determining the tasks for which his talents may be given their highest and best use.

2. *The principle of appreciation for work well done.* Employees must be made to feel worthwhile and related to the total task. The particular contribution of an employee can be very significant if he knows that the assigned task is truly appreciated and is in the spectrum of the goals of the church.

3. *The principle of a fair day's pay for a fair day's work.* Although it has been demonstrated that employees are not motivated solely by financial incentives, "fair wages" are still quite important. If wages or salaries are considered inadequate or unfair, they do indeed become first importance to the employee, affecting his individual achievement as well as the group effort.

4. *The principle of rewards earned, not given.* "A laborer is worthy of his hire." The opportunity to earn an advance is a highly important source of job satisfaction for most employees. A paternalistic approach of "giving" a raise, or "giving" a holiday with pay, can appear condescending and contribute to negative attitudes.

5. *The principle of fairness and consistent treatment of all employees*. One of the quickest ways to lose the respect of subordinates and to lower the morale of the work group is inconsistency in day-to-day policy and partiality in treatment of one person over another.[15]

Staff evaluations are an excellent tool to determine whether employment policies are fair, job descriptions are accurate, and the staff is working effectively and up to expectations. This process doesn't need to be complicated, intimidating, or exhaustive. The exhibits at the close of this chapter are samples of forms for staff evaluations.

Exhibit 7-2 is commercially available and is suitable for use in a church setting.

Exhibit 7-3 could be used in a church with a multiple pastoral staff situation.

Exhibit 7-4 would be suitable for a more in-depth evaluation of professional staff. The staff person completes the form, and the leader, department head, or other person in authority reviews the results. The information is then compared to the individual's job description or the expectations of the church board as it relates to this person's job performance.

Again, an employee performance review is a valuable tool in determining mutual responsibilities, expectations, and proper job fit. In my opinion, a staff member is done a disservice when the reviewer consistently gives a maximum score on the evaluation. Aside from the obvious fact that no one is perfect and everyone has room to grow, it also tells a lot about the manager style and perhaps the desire of the manager to be liked and popular. For a performance review to be effective, there must be honesty and objectivity.

To sum up, the managing of human resources—people—in the context of the local church needs to be done with care, concern, and a desire to do what is right. Personnel policies and performance evaluations need to be firm but fair. The entire matter of proper stewardship permeates this issue. Since a great deal of the church's resources are spent in this area, there is—before God—a considerable responsibility.

Many of these dedicated people have either given up more lucrative opportunities in secular fields or they have simply chosen to work at a church out of a desire to advance Christ's kingdom. Whatever the motivation, the church should set an example to reward these workers who are worthy of hire.

---

15. Adapted from Robert N. Gray, *Managing the Church*, National Institute of Church Management (New York: NCC Publication Service, 1977).

FAITH EVANGELICAL CHURCH SUPPORT STAFF
Job Description

Job Title:
Department:

Job Relationships:
  Supervised by:
  Supervises:

POSITION SUMMARY:

DUTIES & RESPONSIBILITIES:

QUALIFICATIONS:
Education & experience:

Knowledge, skills and abilities:

Working conditions:

Exhibit 7-1

EMPLOYEE PERFORMANCE EVALUATION

Name _____ Date_____

Dept. _____ Job Title_____

Check one:　　□ Annual　　□ New Employee　　□ Termination　　□ Other _____

Date of Last Review:_____ Date Employee Began Present Position: _____

Next Scheduled Review: _____

See rating information (Part III) on reverse side of this form.	U	F	S	G	E	Comments
1. Job Understanding: Employee possesses a clear knowledge of the responsibilities and the task he or she must perform.						
2. Job Performance: The neatness, thoroughness and accuracy of employee's work.						
3. Job Productivity: The quality of the employee's work in terms of volume and accomplishments.						
4. Dependability: Can you rely upon this individual in terms of being on time and completion of tasks.						
5. Cooperation: The ability to work willingly with associates, subordinates, supervisors and others.						
6. Overall Rating						

7. General comments as to employee's strengths, weaknesses and action taken to improve job performance _____

_____

_____

_____

_____

_____

Supervisor_____ Reviewing Officer_____

Date _____ Date_____

Has this report been discussed with employee?　　□ Yes

　　　　　　　　　　　　　　　　　　　　　　　　□ No, if not why? _____

　　　　　　　　　　　　　　　　　　　　　　　　_____

　　　　　　　　　　　　　　　　　　　　　　　　□ If yes, note employee's comments _____

　　　　　　　　　　　　　　　　　　　　　　　　_____

　　　　　　　　　　　　　　　　　　　　　　　　_____

_____ Date Reviewed with Employee _____
Employee's Signature

Exhibit 7-2

PASTORAL IMPACT EFFECTIVENESS SHEET
Grace Community Church

Please write in the appropriate number of 1 to 5
(Minimal or Weak — 1 2 3 4 5 — Maximal or Strong)

NAME	IMPACT FACTORS 0	1	2	3	4	5	Ttl.	NAME	IMPACT FACTORS 0	1	2	3	4	5	Ttl.

PASTORAL IMPACT FACTORS

CONSIDERATIONS

1 RESPONSIBILITY — The number of people involved in leadership & ministry, & the number of people directly & significantly influenced by this ministry..

2 REPLACEABILITY — The degree of difficulty in replacing this person in this ministry..

3 TEAM — The degree of interfacing, contributing to and mutually supporting other ministries at Grace..

4 QUALITY — The degree of effectiveness in the following: discipleship and leadership development; evangelization, edification & equipping; creativity & innovation; excitement, dedication & confidence engendered in those involved..

5 THRUST — The degree of significance & necessity this ministry has on the thrust of Grace Church specifically & the Kingdom in general..

0 THE COMBINED WEIGHT — given to years on Grace staff, degrees, background & experience. . .

Exhibit 7-3

MINISTRY PROFILE

==

Below, list any special goals or projects
currently being worked on, over and above
normal responsibilities. (Such as articles
being written, curriculum, studies, etc.)

Special comments

==

1.

_____

2.

_____

3.

_____

4.

_____

5.

_____

6.

_____

Exhibit 7-4

Facilities Management

An empty stable stays clean—but there is no income from an empty stable" (Proverbs 14:4, TLB*). If you apply that verse to church facilities, you could say, "If we could just lock all the Sunday school classrooms, the kids wouldn't mess them up!"

Obviously, that isn't a practical solution to managing facilities in a local church. Caring for facilities in today's church requires skill, creativity, hard work, and in some cases a great deal of diplomacy. Properly managing a church's buildings and grounds is an area that presents unique situations to each church.

Scheduling

The issue of scheduling is a logical place to start. As mentioned before, we could simply shut the buildings down and lock the doors to save money, along with wear and tear. If you pursue that notion to its logical end, then why have buildings at all?

In dealing with the issue of scheduling, it is best to have one central church calendar. There should also be one person who is designated "keeper of the calendar." This individual should be a "people person" and be firm but fair (objective, not playing favorites). Many churches reproduce their calendars and have them distributed on a periodic basis—weekly, biweekly, or monthly. It is not uncommon even to publish a three-month calendar.

An easy way to help people get room reservations on the calendar is to provide a simple sign-up form. The form should be uncomplicated yet inclusive. Above all, it should be in at least two parts—a copy for the church and one for the member. A sample form is provided at the end of this section. (See Exhibit 8-1.)

*The Living Bible.

The calendar contact person should communicate frequently with the head custodian. A room may be in need of repair, and you certainly don't want activities planned in a room when that room is being painted.

Usage

Every church should have a basic set of guiding principles relating to the use of its facilities. Time, setting, and proximity are to be considered in the overall policy and scheduling process.

Time

The time of day is important because it may affect other activities. What other similar or conflicting event is taking place at the same time? Scheduling the high school music group and a high school party at the same time hurts both activities.

Setting

The activity needs to be appropriate to the room or setting. You don't want an exuberant junior high party in the sanctuary or a pie-eating contest on a carpeted area (if possible). Appropriateness has to do with both taste and the potential mess likely to result from the activity.

Proximity

Having a band performing in a room next to the monthly Board of Elders meeting is not an example of good scheduling. Although this is an extreme example, it is an illustration of the importance of proximity. The basic principle, therefore, is simply to make sure the time of day, the appropriateness of the setting, and the proximity to other groups is correct.

Maintenance

Once again, many maintenance issues relate specifically to each church and its buildings. But as in the case of scheduling and usage, there are some standard guidelines.

It is possible to be creative in this area as well. For instance, does your church use its own people for maintenance and custodial work, or is it possible to contract it out? Another overall question would be, Do we want to hire people who are generalists, the "handyman" type of person, or do we focus on bringing in specialists to care for our buildings? Most churches cannot afford a staff of specialists, so they stay with a man with overall skills and call in a specialist when it is necessary. Electrical, heating, air conditioning, plumbing, and some construction work often are done by outside contractors.

The same is true for custodial services. Many churches contract this out in order to avoid the cost of maintaining their own staff. The exception, however, is those churches that require multiple room setups and teardowns. Most custodial services will not set up chairs, platforms, podiums, microphones, and so on. It is usually best to hire your own people on a limited basis to perform these tasks and definitely to be available on Sundays.

Finally, the maintenance and care of buildings over the long haul is performed better if there is a scheduled routine. Churches with large facilities should rotate the carpet care and other ongoing routine maintenance on a periodic basis. There is always maintenance and upkeep work to be done on church facilities. A request for maintenance work should be submitted in writing and properly scheduled. (See Exhibits 8-2 and 8-3.)

Building Security

This has become a matter of great importance to most churches today. Unfortunately, churches have been notoriously poor at dealing with this issue. Some are learning the hard way that a church is an easy target for crime and vandalism. Generally thieves go after money, computers, office machines, sound equipment, anything that is portable and can be sold quickly. There is even an increase in malicious vandalism directed at churches in many areas of the country.

Because a church is a somewhat public building, it is difficult to have high security measures. ID badges and coded access doors with closed circuit cameras aren't always appropriate. So a good philosophy is, "If it isn't nailed down, you better lock it up!"

Many churches today are scheduling much of their custodial work at night. For example, two shifts can be scheduled: 3-11 and 11-7. This allows the work to be accomplished when the buildings are empty. Further, the activity, with lights going on and off in different buildings during the night, provides a sense of security. Many churches are also using drive-by security services to check buildings and locks and even to ask the identification of people wandering around the buildings after hours. The goal is to have the church either look busy or be under surveillance as much as possible.

If that is not practical, install electronic measures to secure your buildings with window tapes, magnetic threshold contacts, motion detection, and heat sensing devices. There are even churches that hire their own guards to walk "a beat" and keep an eye on buildings and grounds at night.

A further protective measure has to do with the issuing of keys. In many churches that can be a political "hot potato." However, everyone doesn't need to have access to buildings. Perhaps the best policy is to have your church's ruling board decide which people should get keys. Letting the board make this decision removes that burden from the senior pastor, church employees, or individual members.

Property Liability

In today's society, this is one area where your church could be financially wiped out in a very brief time. It isn't wise to cut corners when it comes to purchasing liability insurance. Needless to say, you would want to insure the buildings and contents for their replacement value as well as to identify the more significant areas of risk to your church property. There are many instances in which churches have discovered that their property was under-insured after a loss, resulting in a great deal of out-of-pocket expense. Once again, your chances of a loss from theft are significant, the reason being that a church is a somewhat public building with easy access and many visitors.

Another high-risk area involves injuries occurring on your property. Although this may seem like a legal matter and not a facilities issue, any hazard within reason that could cause an injury should be removed (see section 9). Special attention should be given to athletic events because the potential for injury increases, especially when equipment is poorly maintained or there are hazards present. Experience has shown that in today's environment some people will not hesitate to sue a church if they are injured.

Built for a Purpose

Finally, remember that church buildings belong to God and His people. They should be utilized to their fullest, keeping in mind the appropriateness and the need for balanced schedules. Just as an airplane was designed and built to fly, our church facilities must also fully meet their intended use and purpose—to help advance Christ's kingdom.

Room Number	**ACTIVITY & CALENDAR REQUEST**
	FACILITY RESERVATION

Name of activity _____

Date of function _____ From (am/pm) _____ To (am/pm) _____

Name of group_____ Contact Person_____

Phone (home) _____ (work)_____

Address _____ City_____ Zip _____

Number of people expected _____ Dept. head approval _____

Nursery care needed: yes/no   Bulletin announcement needed: yes/no

Reservations (tickets) needed: yes/no

Where _____ Cost $ _____ Deadline _____

Audio-Visual equipment needed _____

Other equipment needed _____

Food or refreshments served _____

VEHICLE REQUEST

Name of Group _____ Function _____

Destination _____

Van # _____ Date needed _____

Time (leaving) _____ (returning) _____

Program leaders are responsible for getting drivers, vehicle inspection forms, medical/liability consent forms, and van keys.

Use below for Room Set Up Diagram

MASTER CALENDAR

Today's Date _____

Time_____

Initials_____

White and yellow copies to Facilities Director; pink copy to Receptionist.

Exhibit 8-1

FIRST CHRISTIAN CHURCH
WORK ORDER REQUEST

(Complete and submit to church office)

Requested by:_____ Dept.:_____ Date: _____

Room/Area where work is to be performed: _____

Description of services requested:* _____

_____

_____

Use the back for further description or illustration.

Work performed _____

_____

Signature:_____

For Office Use Only	
Material charge: _____	G/L #: _____
Manhours to complete: _____	Date completed: _____

Exhibit 8-2

	Time	Job #	Description of services requested:	✔
Custodial Maintenance Daily Worksheet		by: _____	Date: _____	
1.				
2.				
3.				
4.				
5.				
6.				
7.				
8.				
9.				
10.				
11.				
12.				
13.				
14.				
15.				
16.				
17.				
18.				
19.				
20.				

NOTES

Exhibit 8-3

Managing the Risks

Many church members don't give much thought to the potential liability risks in their own church. After all, who would sue a church? On the other hand, since the American Bar Association in 1990 conducted workshops on how to sue churches and clergy members, local church congregations need to sit up and take notice. Religious organizations are no longer off-limits when it comes to lawsuits and liability injuries.[16]

Is your church financially protected if any of the following events should occur?

- Your building is damaged by fire
- An attender is hurt on your property
- An employee steals office equipment
- A car drives through your front doors
- The church treasurer embezzles a large sum of money
- A church employee is hurt on the job
- The church is burglarized
- The senior pastor dies

What would you do? The usual answer is, "Call our insurance agent." That is, of course, assuming you have insurance covering any or all of these claims. Relying on insurance is only one of many remedies.

Risk Management

There are four ways a church can cope with the possibility of claims arising from injury or other forms of liability.

16. Steve Levicoff (*Christian Counseling and the Law* [Chicago: Moody, 1991]) has written a good resource book for churches concerning contemporary legal realities.

Eliminate the Risk

It is possible to totally eliminate certain, specific risks. These could be related to employees using inferior materials or unsafe equipment. Moreover, perhaps your buildings are designed with hazardous walkways, low clearances, slippery surfaces, or other dangers. Then there are always the well-known hazards of faulty wiring, exposed steam pipes, broken stairs, and other areas demonstrating clear negligence. A church, like any other organization, risks the possibility of injuries and liability by not identifying and eliminating these problems. If church leaders don't take these potential hazards seriously, they could be exposed to lawsuits and, in some instances, could be criminally liable. Furthermore, gross negligence or flagrant violations of health and safety standards is sufficient cause for an insurance carrier to void and cancel your policy.

Lower the Risks

From a practical standpoint, it would be impossible to eliminate every risk, even if you knew where they were. So, short of total removal, the next best thing is to reduce the risks. Take a close, critical look at your church buildings and grounds to determine what, if anything, can be done to lessen possible hazards. What precautionary steps can be taken to reduce your exposure in these areas?

For instance, the danger of falling off a ladder cannot be eliminated; but the use of safety ladders with guardrails on either side can reduce the risk. Hallways need to be free of obstacles; walkways should be clear of electrical cords (overhead projector operators take note!). Having a good policy regarding the issuing of keys to buildings and protecting computers and office equipment from being carried away are examples of ways to reduce risks.

Accepting the Risks

Self-insurance has been suggested in the past as one method whereby a church can create a contingency fund to pay for claims, instead of paying liability insurance premiums. Although that may have been an option in the past, it is no longer practical. The cost of legal fees plus the size of a possible judgment make the practice of "going bare" totally impractical. Given high replacement costs for buildings, furniture, and fixtures, as well as the staggering amounts of some judgment claims, a church could be totally wiped out with one incident.

Accepting the risk can be appropriate when the risk cannot be totally eliminated or the cost of insurance is prohibitive. As any insurance agent will tell you, it is possible to buy insurance for almost every conceivable risk. But that simply isn't practical for most churches.

Furthermore, there are situations where, even though the church carries coverage for a specific risk, it may be advisable to go ahead and pay the damages. This applies when there is a likelihood that your premiums will increase significantly as a result of the incident or when the costs of the claim are within the policy's deductible portion.

Shifting the Risk

Purchasing insurance coverage enables the church to transfer its risks. In effect, when you buy insurance, you agree to absorb some of the smaller, periodic losses in the form of premiums and deductibles in exchange for avoiding the large, uncertain claims.

Types of Insurance

Fire Insurance

Most standard fire insurance policies cover the buildings, the property contained within them, and property temporarily removed from them because of fire or lightning. Normally, this coverage does not extend to accounting records, bills, deeds, money, securities, windstorms, hail, smoke, explosions, vandalism, automatic sprinkler leakage, or malicious mischief. A church needs additional coverage to guard against these losses. Fires resulting from a war or actions taken under the orders of a civil authority are not covered by insurance.

In order to keep your fire insurance policy valid, it is the church's responsibility to take every reasonable precaution to protect its property both before and after a fire. Aside from inspecting facilities for fire hazards, church leaders need to be aware of the type of activities going on in their buildings. Having an indoor barbecue, using unprotected candles, and cooking on a hot plate or a faulty pilot light are examples of preventable risks. Negligent acts such as renting your facility out to people who are neglectful or engage in reckless activities could void your coverage.

Liability Insurance

Church leaders are responsible for the safety of church employees as well as the attenders. Most liability policies cover losses stemming from bodily injury or property damage claims, expenses for medical services required at the time of the accident, investigation, and court costs.

These types of policies will pay claims depending on both the limit per accident and the limit per person provided for in the policy. For example, if your policy has a per-accident limit of $400,000 and a per-person limit of $100,000, and if one person receives a $300,000 judgment against the church, the insurance company will pay only

$100,000. That means the church will be responsible for paying the balance of $200,000 even though it is within the per-accident limit. Needless to say, the operative word here is "caution." In other words, read the fine print as well as the bold print and be sure you agree with any of the limitations in your coverage.

Automobile Insurance

If your church owns one or more vehicles, automobile insurance is essential. Coverage in this area should include the following:

- Bodily injury claims
- Property damage claims
- Medical payments
- Uninsured motorist damages
- Damage to your vehicles
- Towing costs

The cost of coverage normally depends on the value and number of vehicles and the kinds of driving involved (making deliveries, carrying passengers) as well as the location of the church. And of course, the higher the deductible, the lower the premium.

Worker's Compensation Insurance

The laws in every state require employers to (1) provide employees with a safe place to work, (2) hire qualified coworkers, (3) provide a safe work environment and tools, and (4) warn employees of dangerous working conditions. Failure to do this could result in liability damages. It is also quite possible that a worker could be paid for an on-the-job injury the rest of his life.

All churches are subject to worker's compensation laws, and this is not a case of government interference in religious affairs. In fact, it could be viewed as government protecting or absorbing some of the liability risks relating to employee injuries or disabilities. A church especially should want to provide a safe and secure workplace for its employees.

Under worker's compensation insurance, the carrier pays all claims the employer is legally required to pay a claimant. Basic insurance rates are set by law in most states, but a church can still control its premiums to a certain extent. Since rates vary according to the occupational category, make sure all church employees are classified correctly. You do not want an office worker classified along with the higher classified maintenance or custodial person. Another way to lower premiums is to ensure that safety measures are in place to reduce the risk of an accident and possible claim.

Management vs. Stewardship

There are other types of insurance a church may choose to purchase, although these are less significant. They include business interruption insurance, glass insurance, fidelity bonds, crime insurance, and key personnel insurance. A check list of possible coverage is provided for your church to determine if you are adequately insured. (See Exhibit 9-1.)

Some believe that God will protect His church and that, therefore, it isn't necessary to purchase a lot of insurance. The Bible is clear that God does protect His people from a spiritual standpoint. In those instances, however, where God has given a local body of believers facilities and vehicles, He expects the leaders to be good stewards. Throughout the Old Testament, in those instances where God physically protected His people Israel, He still expected their cities to have walls, gates, and armed soldiers. That was the kind of world they lived in and the way they managed risks.

Today, in most locations, our church buildings don't require armed guards posted twenty-four hours a day. However, we make sure that the doors are locked, alarms set, strategic locations are well lit, and liability insurance premiums are paid in full. The world we live in sometimes requires added protection—even for churches. Good risk management is also good stewardship.

Insurance Checklist

Type of insurance	Purchase	Do Not Purchase
Property insurance		
Fire	_____	_____
Windstorm	_____	_____
Hail	_____	_____
Smoke	_____	_____
Explosion	_____	_____
Vandalism	_____	_____
Water damage	_____	_____
Glass	_____	_____
Liability insurance	_____	_____
Workers' compensation	_____	_____
Business interruption	_____	_____
Dishonesty		
Fidelity	_____	_____
Robbery	_____	_____
Burglary	_____	_____
Comprehensive	_____	_____
Personal		
Health	_____	_____
Life	_____	_____
Key personnel	_____	_____

Exhibit 9-1

Is the Way We Give Hurting Our Church?

A note found in the offering plate read, "The enclosed check for $500 is to go toward the purchase of a new church organ." Also, Mr. Green, a regular tither, is now requesting that his weekly gift be sent to the hungry children in Ethiopia. In addition, Joe Youngblood, the youth pastor, received a gift of $100 from an anonymous donor, "In appreciation for your tireless efforts in working with our young people."

All of those gifts are certainly appreciated, but what should church leaders do if they don't need a new organ or know of a way to get money to Ethiopian children? And maybe the youth pastor just got a raise. The church doesn't want to return the gifts, and yet the donors have placed certain conditions on the way church leaders should spend them.

Donations given to the church with specific instructions for their use, commonly known as "designated gifts," cannot quietly be added to the general fund and spent for current needs. Both the Internal Revenue Service and the donor have a legal and moral right to know exactly how a designated gift is spent. Gifts designated for mission projects, "love offerings" for speakers, donations to meet financial needs of church members, and funds given to finance concerts, musicals, films, radio programs, and scholarships for camps and schools all must be carefully accounted for.

Perhaps you like to earmark your giving so that you have control over where it is spent. But place yourself in the position of the church treasurer, who with each designated gift faces a bittersweet dilemma: How can he deal with the gift in a way that is agreeable to the donor, consistent with the purposes of the church, and in keeping with guidelines of the IRS and the principles of wise stewardship?

The wise treasurer asks two sets of questions:

1. Is the direction of this gift in line with the priorities of our church? If not, should we reevaluate our priorities in order to pursue the objective of the giver?

2. If we return the gift, what effect will our refusal have on the donor? How can we best handle our refusal?

If the gift is to an individual on the church staff, two additional concerns need to be addressed.

One has to do with fairness to other church employees. Staff members in positions of high visibility tend to receive more special gifts. But men and women working in support areas will have needs just as great—and possibly even greater, depending on their family situation. Is the church prepared to give them matching gifts?

The second concern is that the donor needs to know that a gift designated to an individual is not tax deductible. The law states, "If contributions . . . are earmarked by a donor for a particular individual, they are treated, in effect, as being gifts to the designated individual and are not deductible."[17] The treasurer may determine that a designated gift cannot be utilized in the way it was intended. As painful as it may be, he must openly and honestly talk to the person offering the gift, tactfully encouraging him to continue in his spirit of generosity by helping the church leaders meet the priorities and goals of the church.

Indeed, a deeper issue is at stake than the legal mechanics of handling designated gifts. The biblical concept of church leadership may be threatened by designated giving. Acts 4:35 sets forth a rather subtle yet profound practice. New Testament believers were truly committed to meeting the needs of others, but, instead of giving gifts directly to certain individuals or special projects, they would lay their gifts "at the apostles' feet; and they would be distributed to each, as any had need."

The apostles were godly men with a proven track record of being good stewards. They were in a position to know the needs and requirements of the local body. As the God-ordained leaders of the body, they determined where and how resources were to be spent. It wasn't a case of a small group of powerful men trying to call all the shots. They were honest, trustworthy men, properly motivated, who knew where and how to get the job done. And the people confidently submitted to their leadership. The modern day application of that first-century practice is threefold.

First, the responsibility of church finances should be placed in the hands of trusted, duly-appointed leaders. Biblical church leadership is not by majority rule. Decisions—financial and otherwise—should be made according to the wisdom of godly church leaders who are charged with the responsibility of overseeing the entire congregation.

17. Internal Revenue Service, Ruling 62-113 (1962).

Second, establish an annual budget that provides funds for all the church ministries—a "unified budget." Here, different ministries are kept separate for internal bookkeeping purposes. The fund for the new organ, the debt reduction funds, the camp scholarship fund, and the myriad of other special emphasis areas that tend to encourage designated giving can be allowed for on a limited basis in this way. If the church leaders recognize a specific area of need, they bring that need before the people of the church to request designated gifts.

Finally, establish a written policy limiting the solicitation and receiving of gifts for designated purposes. A suggested policy might read something like this:

> Contributions will not be received that are designated for organizations or individuals not recognized by the IRS as tax-exempt.
>
> Contributions can be designated for particular purposes, programs, or projects of the church itself, which have been duly authorized in advance as part of its religious activity by the Board of Elders (or your particular ruling body). Expenditures of such contributions for the purposes designated will be entirely within the discretion of the church or its appropriate internal body.
>
> If the church cannot find a way to utilize such contributions within its own purposes and the donor's designation, it will return the donation to the donor with an explanation of the problem.
>
> The church will determine the best means of carrying out its purposes with such contributions. If an outside agency is utilized, the church will continue to exercise expenditure accountability to make sure that its funds are applied to its purpose by any contractor, agent, or grantee.

In the final analysis, the practice of designated giving not only drains away from the church's financial base but also sets up a framework in which people can, in fact, "vote" with their checkbooks. In some situations, the church may be struggling just to pay the light bill or the minister's salary. A new stained-glass window simply may not be one of the pressing priorities. But the decision should be made by the church's spiritual leaders, not the people who have the most money.

Whether you agree or disagree with this approach, it certainly is something to think about!

Hey, Brother,
Can You Spare a Dime?

ormer President Reagan once proposed, "If every church and synagogue in the U.S. would adopt ten poor families beneath the poverty level . . . we could eliminate all government welfare in this country."

Former New York City Mayor Edward Koch asked the 350 churches and synagogues of his city to shelter ten homeless men and women each night. His proposal was criticized by priests, rabbis, and ministers. He received only seven positive replies.

A *Wall Street Journal* article spotlighted the situation. It stated that churches throughout the country face increasing demands to help the impoverished. This dilemma is a growing concern among America's congregations.

The challenge to church leaders is clear: *We need to respond biblically.* We simply cannot sidestep the issue and hope it will go away. It's here—at our doorstep.

Needy people will call the church, arrive in broken-down cars, or walk in the front door. They all have the same request—food, a place to sleep, clothing, or gasoline. There is the young man who comes to the church asking for food and a place to spend the night. Another man in the congregation, who has been unemployed for two months, calls and says his family doesn't have enough food for the week.

Historically, this was once the church's responsibility—providing aid to the poor, aged, and disabled. The church, for whatever reasons, allowed government to take over this burden. Now, because of cuts in various federally funded assistance programs, people are again turning to the church for help.

Although politicians expect churches to care for the needy, most congregations are not prepared to cope. They either have limited resources or simply do not feel obligated to help the poor.

The church has three options:

1. *Help everyone*. Provide food, shelter, and clothing to anyone who can demonstrate an apparent need and then allow God to deal with the question of their "honesty."
2. *Help no one*. The philosophy of "us four—no more—shut the door" is typical in today's churches. Parishioners believe that the problem is beyond the ministry and scope of the local church.
3. *Help the truly needy*. The ideal is to help these people become self-sufficient without creating a dependency on the church or just another welfare system.

In aiding the poor, we need to answer three questions to develop a clear-cut strategy.

Who qualifies for aid?

The Bible classifies two types of individuals. Hebrews 13:2 tells us, "Do not neglect to show hospitality to strangers, for by this some have entertained angels without knowing it."

Also, in 1 John 3:17 we read, "Whoever has the world's goods, and beholds his brother in need and closes his heart against him, how does the love of God abide in him?"

We are responsible to help strangers and those in Christ's Body. In setting priorities, Scripture tells us to "do good to all men, and especially to those who are of the household of the faith" (Galatians 6:10). Our first obligation is to God's redeemed family.

Who do we consider needy?

Generally speaking, we need to respond to those without resources or an immediate ability to help themselves. First Timothy 5:5 describes needy widows as destitute, lacking a means for support. They're the ones devoid of basic necessities, "without clothing and in need of daily food" (James 2:15).

Resources include assistance from family, relatives, and friends (1 Timothy 5:4). Property, savings accounts, cars, television, or any other surplus items can be sold for basic provisions.

People worthy of aid, therefore, are those lacking necessities or the immediate ability to remedy their situation.

To what extent should we meet needs?

The answer, although simple to say, is difficult to implement. We have to meet immediate needs while helping individuals become self-supporting. Giving food without guidance encourages people to return whenever they get hungry. But there are many practical solutions.

Church members can donate nonperishable food items, clothing, and blankets for the needy. Gift certificates purchased from local supermarkets or fast-food restaurants also help.

One way to handle the situation is to allow a person to work for his money. The Bible says if a man won't work, he shouldn't eat (2 Thessalonians 3:10). Handing a man a paint brush or shovel is a sure way to check out his motivation.

The local church can use public agencies, usually funded by private donors, to help those outside its congregation. The Salvation Army, rescue missions, half-way houses, the Travelers Aid Society, and other organizations are equipped to aid the distressed.

When money is given, it must be handled carefully. Cash might not be used for its intended purpose. Examine the genuineness of each person's request.

Since church members have worked hard to earn funds for purchasing provisions, church leaders must guarantee good stewardship. To ensure that you are not being "taken," prepare an interview questionnaire. The guide on the following page is designed to help church leaders determine a person's identity, employment status, possible church affiliation, and any additional resources he may have overlooked.

American churches cannot completely replace the nation's welfare system. Government should not throw its poor on the local church, saying, "Here, we can't afford these people anymore; you take care of them."

We're committed to helping truly needy people so they can eventually help themselves. That includes serving spiritual food as well as physical sustenance. Let's not neglect this aspect of our "aid program" by pouring all our time and resources into only meeting physical needs. Quoting Deuteronomy 8:3, Jesus said, "Man shall not live on bread alone, but on every word that proceeds out of the mouth of God" (Matthew 4:4).

Request for Assistance
Mountain Community Church

1. Are you a church member? If not, how were you referred to us?

2. What is your need? (Please be specific.)

3. Where do your closest relatives live?

4. Do they know about your need?

5. Are you receiving any aid (financially or otherwise) from a government agency (unemployment insurance, social security, worker's compensation)?

6. Have you been employed locally? Where?

7. When and where was the last time you sought employment?

8. Are you willing to work today if we know of an available job?

9. Do you attend church? If so, where?

10. What is your minister's name?

11. Have you sought assistance at any other churches in this area? If so, where?

12. If we are *unable* to help you, what other options do you have?

13. If we are *able* to help you, how many people are involved? (Please list family members, etc.)

14. Do you have some form of identification?

    (Please remember, our church is not a government-assisted agency.
    All available resources are a result of direct donations from our congregation.)

Exhibit 11-1

Worthy Is the Pastor

A recent study points out that the average American pastor with a congregation of three hundred people earns a salary of $17,875.[18] One out of five ministers moonlights to supplement his income. In fact, one study done ten years ago indicated that only 5 percent of American ministers earn more than $22,000 a year, and 14 percent earn less than $10,000.[19]

Low pay for the pastor isn't a new problem. But out of necessity many church governing boards are just now beginning to acknowledge it.

Inadequate income does produce consequences. A pastor who is concerned about providing the basic needs of his own family may not have the emotional energy to concentrate on the needs of his church. Financial burdens may contribute to a lack of enthusiasm, a low self-esteem, and a negative attitude toward the ministry. Ultimately, that will harm the congregation.

The salary pinch is no respecter of age. Many seminary graduates are forced to leave their first pastorate because they cannot support their families at an adequate standard of living. Meanwhile, combined low pay and substandard retirement programs cause some veteran pastors to stay in the ministry long after they should retire. Their fraying health and vigor hurt both themselves and the church.

The apostle Paul wrote to Timothy, "Let the elders who rule well be considered worthy of double honor, especially those who work hard at preaching and teaching. For the Scripture says, 'You shall not muzzle the ox while he is threshing,' and 'The laborer is worthy of his wages'" (1 Timothy 5:17-18).

The phrase "worthy of double honor" does not mean two pats on the back followed by a rousing rendition of "For He's a Jolly Good Fellow." If financial support of

18. Compensation Survey, The National Association of Church Business Administration, Fort Worth, Tex., 1991, p. 152.

19. Brochure published by Presbyterian Minister's Life Insurance Co., 1982.

"honor" is provided to the worthy widow (1 Timothy 5:3), then a double dose is certainly due to the man who is her pastor. Context demands that, just as one provides anongoing reward for the work of an animal, so also should a pastor be adequately compensated for his labor.

The Bible also exhorts us to "appreciate those who diligently labor among you, and have charge over you" (1 Thessalonians 5:12). The phrase "have charge over you" literally means "stand before you." This is best illustrated by a father standing before his family (1 Timothy 3:5); it denotes responsibility, duty, and accountability.

The passage continues: "Esteem them very highly in love because of their work" (1 Thessalonians 5:13). The love mentioned here may well manifest itself through compassionate care, concern, and generosity when it comes time for the annual salary review.

Just as the business community requires an evaluation of anyone in a position of responsibility, so should the church board. A pastor should welcome this as an opportunity to show his church leaders what he really does—long hours of sermon preparation, hospital visitation, counseling, administrative details, late-night phone calls. Shepherding is more than preaching a Sunday message.

A meaningful evaluation will take into consideration the pastor's effectiveness and his contribution to the church's goals. Results of the appraisal should be shared personally with the pastor to help him recognize his strengths as well as his weaknesses. These checkpoints can be used as a beginning:

- *Responsibility*—the number of people under his supervision and the number to whom he ministers
- *Thrust*—the degree of significance, and necessity, of this specific ministry in furthering the total church ministry
- *Replaceability*—the degree of difficulty in replacing the pastor
- *Teamwork*—the degree of interacting with, contributing to, and mutually supporting other ministries
- *Quality*—the degree of effectiveness in: (1) discipleship and leadership development; (2) evangelism, edification and equipping; (3) creativity and innovation; (4) excitement, dedication, and confidence engendered in those involved
- *Qualification*—number of years on church staff, degrees, background, and experience. A point system (e.g., 1-5, with 5 being the best) may offer the best means of "grading" the individual.

One additional factor could also be considered. In the expression "especially those who work hard" (1 Timothy 5:17), the phrase *work hard* comes from the Greek word *kopiaō*, which means "to work hard, toil, labor, strive, struggle; become tired, grow weary."

Apparently, a "sweat factor" should be considered when establishing compensation, particularly in those churches that have multiple staffs with individuals carrying various loads of responsibility. The "up front" leaders are not necessarily the most important. Associate pastors dealing daily with counseling situations, for example, may carry a load just as heavy as senior pastors.

Any pay increase less than the cost of living rate for the previous twelve months should not be considered a raise. On the other hand, keep in mind the local economy, business climate, and financial condition of the church.

A good rule of thumb is to pay the senior pastor the average wage of the church ruling board. Simply ask each leader to submit figures showing his salary plus the value of his benefits. Then add the totals and divide the sum by the number of men participating.

In some situations, outside employment may be a feasible option for supplementing a low salary. Especially in smaller churches, the pastor should be given the freedom to pursue a second job without fear of stigma. Even the apostle Paul worked as a tent maker to avoid placing a financial burden on his local church.

Before allowing the pastor to take that step, however, the church board must honestly determine, "Do we have the resources to assume his full and adequate support?" Sometimes a congregation has more resources than it realizes.

In creating a compensation package, leaders should make every attempt to stretch the dollars as far as they will go. A straight salary isn't the only avenue to explore. With just a little imagination, both the minister and the congregation can benefit.

- *Reimbursement.* The congregation should pay for what it costs to have a pastor. This may involve a car allowance, professional dues, traveling expenses, meals away from home—in other words, the same costs most businesses provide.

- *Benefits.* Any fair compensation package will include health and life insurance. Disability coverage may be added. And a good pension plan should also be provided. All benefits should be furnished to the minister at no cost, thereby allowing him additional tax-free income.

- *Housing.* If the church does not provide a parsonage, a stated housing allowance over and above the pastor's salary should be given. By giving him the opportunity to buy his own home, the congregation helps him build an equity for his future. It is wise to implement the counsel of a church member who knows tax laws. Among other provisions, the Manse Allowance entitlement can be quite beneficial in handling federal taxes and saving taxable dollars.

- *Salary.* Setting a fair salary is the most difficult part of establishing an equitable pay package. A small group of trusted men should consult the pastor, discussing his needs openly, honestly, and lovingly. Future discussion or debate should also be limited to a small group situation.

Many congregations today make a big mistake in committing funds to buildings and programs rather than to people. God does not cause growth through bigger buildings or more programs but through highly motivated individuals who are loved and appreciated by their people. Faithfulness to God's Word and the effective labors of His servants are the keys to growth. Resources should be directed at people first, then programs and facilities.

"Let the church keep the pastor poor and God can keep him humble" is a faulty motto. Most men serving in pulpits today are highly trained, with the majority possessing advanced degrees. In obedience to God, a congregation should pay a minister what he is worth. And God can still keep him humble.

Moody Press, a ministry of the Moody Bible Institute,
is designed for education, evangelization, and edification.
If we may assist you in knowing more about Christ
and the Christian life, please write us without obligation:
Moody Press, c/o MLM, Chicago, Illinois 60610.